D0885044

HOLY WATER, SACRED OIL

THE FOUNTAIN OF YOUTH

Yinergy™

by

C. Norman Shealy, M.D., Ph.D.

Biogenics[R] Books
Fair Grove, Missouri

HOLY WATER, SACRED OIL
THE FOUNTAIN OF YOUTH

Cover by Ann Nunley

Library of Congress Cataloging-in-Publication Data:
Shealy, C. Norman 1932-
Holy Water, Sacred Oil: The Fountain of Youth
Biogenics[R] Books, 2000
ISBN 1-893300-01-3
Library of Congress Number 00 091884

Biogenics[R] Books
5607 S. 222nd Road
Fair Grove, MO 65648
www.selfhealthsystems.com

Printed in the United States of America

Other books, tapes and products by the author available from:

Self-Health Systems
5607 S. 222nd Road
Fair Grove, MO 65648

Phone: 417-267-2900
Fax: 417-267-3102

www.selfhealthsystems.com

info@selfhealthsystems.com

Some substances have multiple names which are equal and interchangeable:

1. Magic Oil, Cell Wellness Restorer™, Crystal Oil and YINERGY™ Oil.

---

2. Magic Water, Prill Water, Crystal Water, Thin Water, Wellness Water.

---

3. Laminar crystals are the mica-like crystals.

DEDICATION

This book is dedicated with love to my wife, Mary-Charlotte who has allowed me the privilege of following my path.

APPRECIATION

Thanks first and foremost to the Wizard, Jim Carter, for reminding me 15 years later that he had discovered "Solid Sunshine." And to my students and patients who so eagerly and freely participated in our experiments on DHEA, magnesium and weight loss. And, of course to Vera Borgmeyer, R.N., M.A., my Research Director who organizes so well. And, of course, to Jody Trotter, who really had to trot to get this done on time.

Cover Designed by
Ann Nunley, M.A.
www.innercounselor.com

TABLE OF CONTENTS

CHAPTER 1

THE SECRET OF LIFE

The search for youth and eternal life is perhaps as old as civilization. Ponce de Leon's worldwide trip to find the Fountain of Youth, the search for the Holy Grail, the alchemist's attempt to convert lead into gold, and most especially, the Philosopher's Stone are all variations of a grand search for the secret of life. The Philosopher's Stone was thought to cure illness, to prolong life, and to bring about spiritual revitalization. It is interesting that in their search for this unknown mystery, evolving alchemists became scientists and out of their work came chemistry, metallurgy, and pharmacology. In the intervening several hundred years, these sciences have dominated the Western world, but in the past decade, even some medical scientists have turned to anti-aging research and others to spiritual revitalization.

Suppose there is a mysterious path to health and longer life? A true Fountain of Youth? Jim Carter is a modern Ponce de Leon, a mystical wizard in search of the Secret of Life. His is a rare tale of intrigue, mystery and to some extent, science fiction so realistic that it sounds like Jules Vern's tales. A little about the background of Jim Carter is in order. He was born in San Francisco Municipal Hospital on December 21, 1947. At that time he lived in Oakland. His father was 48 when Jim was born. Jim has two full sisters and five half brothers and sisters. Jim was the "middle of the second litter." Jim's mother died at age 80 of pernicious anemia. His father died at age 78 of unknown causes. One sister has three Ph.D.'s and was a Professor of Zoology at Maryland State University. The other sister lives in Wisconsin and is married to an engineer of the Burlington Northern Railroad.

Jim says that he never read a book or studied in high school. He "intuited" his way through high school. After that he got interested in reading the Encyclopedia Britannica and has read every issue from 1875 forward. The first one he got was the 1911 edition. It was a "handy" version, 5-1/2 x 9 inches with small print. He read all of 32 volumes and began to run into unusual facts which have long since been "forgotten." As he began reading voraciously these many volumes and many editions of the Encyclopedia Britannica, he began to see changes and noticed that history is always written by the victors and never by the losers. He took a correspondence course from 1876 through the International School in Mining and Metallurgy. By 1980 he became intrigued with the history of mining and he had three of the recipes which had been lost to the mining industry. He learned that he could extract gold when no one else could and over the years, he has supported himself with this. He has used his earnings from mining and refining gold to sponsor the extensive research that he has done with this product.

"THE STONE"

About twenty-six years ago a dear friend gave him a unique piece of stone. In the beginning he thought it was concrete. He was certain it was man-made and there was no doubt that it was "full of magic." There was no "owner's manual" and his friend could offer only two clues to its use and power: "It had a dynamic effect on water and this water had a dynamic effect on plants" and "the secret of this action was Solid Sunshine." The dynamic effect about water was true and he grew his first tomatoes that had a shelf-life of about six months without refrigeration and could be frozen without damage. He was certain of this. The issue of "Solid Sunshine" was another matter that would take nearly eleven years to resolve.

Jim went back to his friend and began putting the pieces to this puzzle together. Mrs. Evans was a "great lady" who had known Jim's family since she and his father went to grammar school in the times of slate and chalk. She could never refuse help to anyone, even those who were coming and going from the ether. The stone had come to her as a repayment of a loan, in fact there were three stones that eventually came to Jim. The loan had been to a retired Federal Judge named Kearns and along with the stones came boxes of esoteric information and the names of a few people who were involved with Kearns. The Quest was on.

The name that appeared most often was that of Swanton, a lawyer and on contacting Mr. Swanton, it became clear that there was much more to the story of the stones. Kearns had a partner named Owen Waltrip and Mr. Waltrip was an engineer for a railroad, not the driver of trains but a tunnel builder. Now in building tunnels through mountains it is not unusual to intersect with caves and sometimes these caves appeared to be "man-made tunnels" themselves. For obvious reasons the railroads seal up these tunnels and do not allow any exploration. In the early 1960's such a tunnel was being built by Waltrip and such an intersection had been discovered and sealed up.

This particular railroad tunnel ran into water and had to be abandoned. Waltrip was at retirement age and he would retire and with his friend Kearns, they reopened the cave and proceeded with what would become a very successful "treasure hunt." What makes this treasure hunt unique, besides the concept of "man-made tunnels" is that Waltrip was an engineer and his hobby was the newly developing science of "solid state electronics." In 1962, solid state systems were laboratory phenomena and Waltrip was a pioneer in this field. What would be recovered was gold and silver metal objects, tablets, and parts of what Waltrip was sure were "solid state machines." Waltrip and Kearns went down into this cave or man-made tunnel and returned with a fortune. They resealed the entrance and knew that whenever they wanted they could come "back to their bank."

Introducing himself to Mr. Swanton, who had been their lawyer for nearly ten years, did not instantly open any doors for Jim. When Jim told Swanton that he had the stones, they began to talk. Swanton had joined Waltrip and Kearns during the first year after their TREASURE had been found. Money was no object. The stories began with "black Cadillacs" and hundred mile per hour trips across the mountains. When the money ran low, Waltrip and Kearns returned to the tunnel to find it flooded. The bank had literally "gone under." Swanton had a "full wall" of file cabinets that told the stories of the years to follow. There were stories of "world class" industrial events that were powered by the "magic of the stones" and the unending litigation between Waltrip, Kearns, and vested interests that were offended by new or perhaps "very old" technology. At any rate, they had built a water purification plant suitable to supply the city of Detroit, apparently succeeded in using common water as a fuel, and finally built a plant to rehydrate coal into fuel that produced four times the B.T.U.'s of the original coal and had no environmental impact, and the MAGIC INGREDIENT IN ALL THESE EVENTS was the stones. See at the end of this chapter summaries of two patents issued to Waltrip which confirm this part of the story very nicely.

INTRIGUE AND THE MAFIA

It is important at this point to provide you with other details of the Waltrip - Kearns connection which I obtained from Bob F. (This is a pseudonym and you can understand as you read his strange story why he has declined having his name used.)

I spent a fascinating afternoon with this delightful 77 year old gentleman. Bob F. worked for an aerospace company in Sacramento, California where he was a master welder. There he met John Stacken from Nebraska who was an excellent machinist, in fact the best that Bob F. ever met. A nephew of Stacken, Nyfert, had met Owen Waltrip who wanted to explore some very unusual concepts and needed a team. Both Stacken and Bob F. were doing "bootleg stuff." That means they did not have government clearance but actually worked on projects for the military which were behind schedule. Stacken came to Bob F. and said, "We may not make much money out of this project but my nephew wants to talk with you." The deal was put together between Nyfert, Stacken, Whaley, and Bob F. which included the concept that if Waltrip's team made money in a big way, all would share in the results. The fourth person, Whaley, was extremely sharp in electronics. Stacken and Bob F. did the welding and machine tooling and Whaley did the electronics. Nyfert was apparently the major organizer.

Several months into the project Bob F. met Waltrip for the first time. He says that Waltrip was not easy to figure out. He would come up with an idea but depended on the four of them to set it up. The three engineers behind the project, John, Bob F., and Whaley put together a piece of equipment about four feet wide and ten inches high. On the bottom, water ran down a chute and across a flat surface of lead. The top was stainless steel plates. By feeding a DC current with an AC carrier they were able to extract metals from water.

The plates could be moved up and down depending upon the size of the flow and the amount of current desired. They set up a plant on the American River near Sacramento. The stainless steel plates would pick up, out of the water, "colloidal gold" and turn the stainless steel plates yellow but when they reversed the polarity to remove the gold, it disappeared. They then went to a flocculation procedure and the water would turn yellow and they could then skim it off with a cloth through the sluice box. The cloth would be yellow but when they tried to use mercury to extract the gold, the cloth would turn yellow but they couldn't get any gold out. Instead, they got platinum, the "wild metal." Interestingly they also found that they had to do the extraction under either a full or new moon. That was the only time they could get the platinum to come out. Bob F. was told that they ended up with two 65 lbs. bars of platinum but he never saw the bars or any money from them. This was about in 1963.

Around that time, the Robertson Sand and Gravel Company was extracting sand and gravel from the river and got in trouble with the State of California's water pollution division and the four originators of the equipment got together and ran the dirty water of the river through their equipment and the water came out crystal clear. The State of California apparently told Robertson that he could continue his operation as long as he would clean up the water and he ran it for some five or six years but was never making any platinum as far as Bob F. knows.

In 1968 a Harold S. came down and Bob F. was told that they had a job up in the Yukon for a major British mining company. The four original team went to the Yukon and apparently they were able to extract gold or platinum there. Two lawyers, Waltrip's lawyer named Kennedy, and another one the name of whom Bob F. cannot remember, put together a contract. The "other" attorney from San Francisco was a tax attorney with great repute, charging even at that date $500 just for a minimal discussion. In the Yukon they set up and ran and collected many barrels of a concentrated black sand (could this be the gold iodide we will talk about later). Harold S. brought all of that down to Sacramento in the winter. Suddenly Waltrip brought in a man named

10

K - and things went hush, hush.

Nyfert was in on the signing of a contract and went to the office of the attorney in San Francisco. Nyfert was apparently extremely intuitive and he intuited that the check for $250,000 that was being offered for some portion of the ownership of the equipment was not a legitimate check. He refused to sign the contract, checked with the bank and found that no such money was available there so the four original builders of the equipment refused to sign a contract. Fortunately Bob F. had insisted that Whaley build into the equipment a secret with requirements of double-switching so that anyone who did not really know the equipment would not be able to make it run. About this time as they were supposedly extracting platinum and possibly gold from the black sand and/or the water, Nelson Rockefeller was brought into the deal and Waltrip was trying to get Nelson Rockefeller to pay $35 million for the process. Rockefeller's engineers watched the equipment running and his engineers told him "anybody can do that. We do it all the time. Why pay $35 million?" Apparently, the story is that Rockefeller went back to New York where he had a contract for $1 billion to clean up the Hudson River. He spent some $200 million but could never make it work, the reason being the secret switches that only Whaley and the inside group of four knew about.

During all of this time, it appeared to Bob F. and the other three in his group that Waltrip was carrying on a lot of double dealing behind their backs.

There were rumors of the Mafia being involved although Bob F. is not certain; but on one occasion when he and his three colleagues were working on a water project in Colorado, "a bunch of guys came out of the woods with shotguns and said they were taking over." At the end of his association with the Waltrip team, K - who had been brought in by Waltrip, discharged the four original builders of the equipment apparently because they were near a profitable venture. Nothing ever was able to be done with it after that because no one but Whaley and his three colleagues knew about the secret switches!

Bob F. says he has no hard feelings about the whole thing. "The way I look at it, everything that goes around comes around. If you treat people right, you will be treated right." Obviously the entire project with Waltrip APPEARS not to have been treating some people right!

During his years of working around mines in the West, Bob F. also met a really wonderful man, a geologist with several generations of geologists in his family, who taught Bob F. that every mineral affects and changes the color of the trees which grow on top of it and Bob F. eventually was able to see that for himself. This, of course, is very interesting because mineral content of the earth varies very considerably as you will see in our chapter on magnesium.

Meanwhile, let us take our story back to that of Jim Carter. Jim came into this well after Bob F. had been excluded from the project. Jim continued to encounter various people who had been associated with Waltrip and Kearns.

Jim had accumulated some very interesting stories. It was clear that the difference between this event and other "treasure hunts" or "Archeological episodes" was that this time the parties involved had a background in physical science. Jim still did not know what was meant by "solid sunshine" or have any clue as to what made the stones work. In the early 1980's he broke one of the stones into many pieces and sent them to as many colleges and testing laboratories as he could get to examine them. The net of this exercise was as many different opinions as there were examiners. Then he talked to people at the Field Museum in Chicago, who said if he would bring in the stones, they would compare them with other artifacts and do a carbon dating.

Three days in Chicago and Jim was "cooking." Not only were his stones over 5,000 years old, but they were part of a CLASS OF ARTIFACT that had been found all over the world. Even more, and this was the big one, the little stones were made of the same material as the "Casing stone" of the Great Pyramid and the ritual founts of the Early Catholic Church. Jim had been given part of an ancient "solid state" technology that was in use before the "flood of Noah." Thousands of similar artifacts had been found and the net result was the assumption that 6,000 years ago, people knew how to make very good concrete. Despite having the makings of a second book, Jim still did not know what "solid sunshine" was or what made the stones work.

In 1988, Jim was working with a friend in Montrose, Colorado. There were two interesting and phenomenal stories that the people of this area liked to relate. The first was of a "silver mining" camp where an interesting spring water had caused those who drank it to develop the power to levitate. This was a little too far out, even for Jim. The second was called the "San Juan Weather Phenomenon" and has been the subject of study by the best meteorologists for the last fifty years. Basically it goes like this: The major storms that impact the midwest and East form over a spot in the "San Juan Mountains."

Jim's work location looked right at the San Juan Range. One very clear day as the sun was setting, Jim noticed a small cloud that seemed to appear from nowhere. In a matter of a couple of hours, this cloud grew until the whole sky was clouds and in the days that followed this "storm" pounded the Midwest. A few weeks later it happened again. This time Jim drove to the location of the forming cloud and on climbing to the top of a relatively small mountain, he found himself looking up at blue sky through a hole in a rotating, and forming storm. He also found himself standing on a mountain of material that was very similar to his stones. His stones changed the character of a barrel of water. What happened when a mountain of this material impacted the water of the atmosphere? "Well, it was called the San Juan Phenomenon." Jim had book three but this time he connected the event with its cause!

The little stones were very similar to concrete, only much stronger. Scattered in this "concrete-like matrix" was a laminar crystal. It was the same with the stone of the mountain, only the laminar crystals were much larger. Here is where it all began to jell. The crystals of the mountain had the same effect on water as the stone. He had found the "solid sunshine." He still did not know how it worked but he did know what was doing the work.

The impact on water was dynamic. Contact with what had now become known as "The Crystal" changed the thickness of common water into the character of a very thin Oil. This altered water not only had a remarkable impact on plant growth, it also was very healing to the skin of people. Just to give you one example: The stone or a small amount of "The Crystal" in a swimming pool, even in 110 degree desert sun, prevented those who used the pool from receiving a sunburn, even after eight hours of exposure. Even more, a person who had been at the lake all day and was burnt to a crisp, would be instantly soothed and totally healed in a matter of minutes from the water in the pool. This he now called "Crystal Magic Water."

Eleven years after the gift, Jim had found that the little laminar plates in the magic stone were capable of changing common water into other forms. The magic of the stone was really the way NATURE DID HER basic business; a law of nature. Was the missing link in our understanding of nature the fact that WATER CHANGES? Could we have entirely missed the "forest for the trees?"

This was the 1980's. We had split the atom. We had gone to the Moon. Man had conquered the world and was learning the absolute lesson of all great conquerors: When the wars are over and there is no one left to steal from you, you still have to EAT, DRINK

AND BREATHE.

If it was true that water could change or be changed into distinct PHASES then it could also be true that the origin of matter was better defined by the Book of Genesis than by our highly advanced convention of science.

Thanks to a 5,000 plus year old artifact, Jim was now completely at odds with virtually every scientist in the world. If what he had discovered was true even in the slightest degree, the leaders of science were not going to be happy to hear about it. After all, they had paid a lot of money for their educations and Jim had barely escaped from high school.

In 1984, everything was still phenomenal. Jim had used the stone and now the crystal to thicken water to the point of it being an Oil (Magic Oil) then a Wax (yet unnamed and still unavailable) and finally heated it to produce a solid (the Crystal). He had taken more water and this newly generated solid and repeated the cycle. He did know that the "solid sunshine" was an operative part of nature. He could mine the Crystal from the mountain in Colorado or he could make it by duplication from common water and he had at least ten major storms a year to keep his attention. He had become an apprentice and the master had died before the flood of Noah. He was learning lots of new scientific terms as he contacted "triple Ph.D.'s and Nobel Prize Winners." Highly scientific terms and phrases like: "Foo Foo," Lunatic, Space Cadet, and many more. Stories like those of Henry Ford driving to work and being fired because he had made a car, were his companions. Thoughts like: I have been given a "Bic Lighter" in a world that has yet to discover fire floated in his mind as he received a load of new scientific jargon from those people who "should have had all the answers."

We had worn out the 1980's and by the 1990's Jim had developed enough practical evidence and learned to use "foo foo" and "lunatic" in the proper context, so that he could at least talk to the KEEPERS OF WISDOM without hurting their feelings. In the 60's we were faced with the threat of nuclear war and the warning of "failing water supplies." By the 70's it was clear that food "would never be used as a weapon" and those who died

of starvation were no longer an issue. By the 80's
bottled water had become a more important subject than
nuclear war and we had achieved the conviction that
unless we learned to "car pool" we would surely have to
use respirators by the year 2000. A new refrigerant had
been discovered and fluorocarbons had been blamed for
the destruction of the environment. We were into the
1990's and it was becoming clear that the solution to our
failing environment was going to either require "alien
intervention" or the "second coming of Christ." By this
time, Jim's options were getting better. He could not
qualify as the representative of an advanced "alien"
civilization and anyway there were already thousands of
applicants for this position. Obviously he was not the
reincarnated Christ, and if he was, there was no reason to
expect a different reception than he received 2000 years
ago, which was enough to keep even a lunatic from
seeking that job! There was, however, another hope. It
seems that if you get a hundred monkeys together, some
kind of magical enlightenment takes place and all these
monkeys become extremely smart. Jim wondered, "I
could be the monkey with the Bic Lighter." All he had

to do was burn 99 other monkeys and they became very smart, the "triple Ph.D.'s and Nobel Prize Winners" would come and round up the monkeys and dissect them, finding out what caused all the screeching and with this information, THEY COULD SURELY SAVE THE WORLD.

The plan was good but there was a flaw. He did not have access to monkeys and the ones that he did know about were already scheduled for dissection to prove some other theory. Now he knew that a hundred monkeys qualified, so he thought maybe a thousand people would have the same effect. The attention span was much shorter than that of a monkey, and they were much more dangerous to work with, but they did make almost the same noise when they were burnt, and it did not require a "triple Ph.D." in order to get them to submit to dissection. Even better, the monkeys cost money and people would pay for the same experience.

THE CRYSTAL

So in 1991, Jim began making his version of the "Bic" and giving it to people so that they could have their experience. He cast the Crystal into a ceramic matrix. He used a cup cake tin to make the plaster molds which he still has. He called these little ceramic cup cakes "Water Pearls" and over a year he produced and gave away nearly 2000 pieces to over 1800 people. They put them in water and drank it or used it to treat all manner of ailments. The response was wonderful. It was obvious that these people had become enlightened, because when the only monkey in this experiment began explaining, it seemed like "MAGIC" that caused the wonderful effect that everyone was so excited about. These people had all learned the highly scientific words that were commonly used in discussions with "triple Ph.D.'s" or "Nobel Prize" winners. He was teaching the world to use "foo foo," "lunatic" and "space cadet" outside the sacred "halls of science."

It was at this point that Jim decided that the problem must be due to the shape of the "Water Pearl." It is really hard to accept that a ceramic cup cake has any particular magic power. So he stopped making cup cakes and started using the ceramic with the crystal to make various shapes: Bowls, Pitchers and Vases. His family cat still drinks from the first bowl he made and she would say it is still remarkable. These things were pretty and there was excitement. The bowl was being called the "Grail" which was really pumping Jim's ego, which his wife assures him that he has. The water from the pitchers was being used to rehydrate orange juice, apple juice, etc., producing juices that were as good as those from tree ripened fruit. Flowers placed in the vase continued through their growth cycle and even produced viable seed or root. This was magic. The monkeys were dancing and Jim could explain the effect as magic and everyone believed him. This was a lot of work but he soon solved this by letting everyone make their own. He had plenty of people who knew how to do ceramics and all he had to do was mix the crystal into the ceramic bisque. Everyone was making bowls, pitchers, vases, but something was wrong. As mentioned before, "this quest has been loaded with phenomena" and magic. It has also always been influenced by what Jim's wife calls ego. Anyway, the ceramics made by these people did not generate the calls of praise and wonderment. In fact, in a little while people quit showing up to get the ceramic crystal mixture. Something was seriously wrong and since the ceramic pieces Jim personally made still performed their magic, he came to the conclusion that HE WAS THE MAGIC INGREDIENT. Something caused Jim to overlook the obvious. The ceramics made with the crystal have a huge shrinkage factor and if you don't leave the kiln closed until they are room temperature, this shrinkage will crack the glaze and this is what holds the water in. No, Jim was not the "chosen one" or the "second coming," it was just that everyone was PEEKING. Everyone was opening their kilns before they were cold and their creations were leaking. If Jim was adding anything personal to the equation, it was just that his "Phlegmatic Personality" was too lazy to look at his creations before they were completely cooled. This whole episode ground to a halt because when people said the "CRYSTAL CERAMICS DID NOT WORK" he did not know they meant they would not hold water. He was back dealing with the "triple Ph.D.'s" and "Nobel Prize Winners." The monkeys had all gone to play with someone else, and it was not until a year or so later that Jim discovered the root of the problem.

PAIN RELIEF

Jim had moved from Springfield, Missouri to Boulder City, Nevada in August of 1991. The previous event took place after he had given up living where palm trees would not grow. Anyway, six months after Jim and his wife escaped the cold, they were given a late in life child, a granddaughter that had just turned six years old. This wonderful little bundle of energy came to visit for a month, SIX AND A HALF YEARS AGO. There are four steps going from the driveway into Jim's house. Picture if you will a sixty pound baby being carried up these steps as she slept. Now, picture her deciding to change shoulders in mid stride. The sound of vertebrae slamming into each other must be among the ten most unique noises in the world. Jim had his first grandparent "sports injury." Every week for the next several months he incorporated a trip to the local osteopath which gained Jim several precious hours of relief from the pain. Jim had made numerous ceramic pieces in practically any shape you can imagine, and some of those who had used them quoted pain relief as one of the attributes. Jim suffered with this chronic and persistent pain for nearly six months, burned out several million brain cells with pain relievers before he was driven to try something that had never failed him in twenty years. So one night as he was lying in agony waiting for the hour or so of sleep that he had become accustomed to, he laid one of the longer ceramic pieces across his hip bones. In a matter of minutes the pain was gone and he wakened eight hours later with the ceramic still in place. This would be a good place for some highly scientific phrases and words if it were not for the rest of the story.

If you haven't guessed, there is one more round of trying for a mass enlightenment effect. This time it is monkeys and mattresses. For the next several days, the ceramic piece offered continuing relief. Sleeping flat on his back was never his choice so it was time to invent another magical device. The "Crystal Sleeper" is just a bag of the laminar Crystal spread evenly on the mattress under the sheet. It had the unique quality of fitting into everyone's lifestyle rather than competing with habits and the time allotted to them. Jim's first experience with the "Crystal Sleeper" was unique. The absence of pain was great and he could sleep in any position but there was another phenomenon. In fact there were many. About 1:00 in the morning he awoke with the sensation that he was freezing to death. He put on more covers and got through the night. The next night he had the same sensation. This time he took his temperature and found that the thermometer did not know he was cold. He began a diary on the third day and in a matter of a week, the cold was no longer an issue. What was happening was the "most vivid three dimensional, full color dreams." They were so totally real that he had total recall of them the following day. And there was another sensation that he coined as "dampening," for the first few hours in the morning he had the feeling that he was slightly perspiring. Six months into this event, he had increased the amount of crystal in the "sleeper" from the original eight pounds to twenty and then to fifty. Each increase had produced the cooling, dampening and the dreams continued to be a nightly theatrical performance. In time he would learn to control the dreams and pass into a real sleep state that most people probably never experience.

Over the next several years, Jim made and gave

over a thousand of these devices to people who had one complaint or another. This time the number of people who wanted them simply outgrew his ability to supply them as gifts. We don't know how many people are required to achieve what can be done with a hundred monkeys. When it got to where he had several hundred people who had complained that they had to smooth this device once a month, he quit.

For eleven years Jim looked for the secret of the stone. Then another twelve years seeking acceptance of what he had found. All the time, even he questioned the obvious power of the Crystal. All the time he was offended by those who would discredit it, because he simply could not accept that "it did not matter how many monkeys you had in the test, if they were in a zoo, the enlightenment would never come." The last few years have been even more dynamic. He found natural sources of the magic things in virtually all its phases and in amounts suitable to change the world. Piece by piece the mysteries became the reality.

Jim can explain why some cultures live "longer than normal lives" and hopefully he can make it possible for you to do the same. Recently he connected the dots in such a way that they intersect with the aspects of convention and because they may help a few other good people, we are merging the ancient science of the stone with the modern need for answers. The magic that may really make your life better begins with "Magic Oil." See the testimonials later. This world is "hot and burning" and all burning is dehydration. Magic Water, either Alpha or Beta, moisturizes and soothes.

The Story of
CELL WELLNESS RESTORER™

If you have read the story of the stone, you probably have some idea of the uniqueness of this entire project. How does a person explain something, i.e. Cell Wellness Restorer or Wellness Water, when there is no peer or comparative? You just tell the story and let everyone come to their own conclusions. Obviously, your personal experience will go a long way towards clearing up many of your questions and as we share experiences, we will all gain more insight. We have been on this quest for a very long time, and we would only hope to tell you that we appreciate you coming on board. The truth is that we are learning right along with you. Every day we hear many stories that are similar to what we have heard before, but every once in a while we are amazed at what is going on. Most of us have always had a desire to live a very long life and to enjoy every minute of it. Wellness is a very serious issue.

Cell Wellness Water was originally named "Magic Water" by Jim's granddaughter; children are really very smart. It is a form of water that is readily accepted by living cells. It is a wonderful moisturizer. If you had enough of the Prills or one of the magic stones, or a supply of the unique Crystal, and you allowed your "Wellness Water" to stay in contact with the influence these substances convey for a longer period of time, you would see your Cell Wellness Water (CWW), first become very thin, about half that of common water, and then become thicker, about like a fine oil. Jim called this second phase "Magic Oil" and now Cell Wellness Restorer (CWR)™.

At any rate, the magic was good enough to gain my attention and with my research, and the input of thousands of users, we put to rest any concerns that these substances could in anyway harm anyone. Now, if Cell Wellness Water and Wellness Restorer could only do good, their merit would have to stand on the "level of good" they could do. Unlike anything else in this world, these products would have to prove themselves to every user by results. Does CWR work? How many success stories would it take, for Cell Wellness Water and Wellness Restorer to get past the point of a phenomenon? Does it really matter what the explanation is if it makes people feel better?

The prophecies that were presented by me in my most recent book, SACRED HEALING, went something like this: These substances were of a sacred nature, I guess calling them Sacred Water or Holy Water would be saying this. The use of "Wellness Water" either in its thin or thick form could dramatically reverse the aging process, and offer hope in what are termed chronic conditions or those conditions that defy most if not all medical approaches. Becoming younger would be the best approach to the issues of destructive aging. Beyond the prophecies, these substances could be and had been proven to cause alteration in body chemistry, and although the alterations were initially different than expected, they did without fail happen and they were without fail accompanied by enhanced states of vitality and general well being.

YINERGY™

Going on with the story. Thin water or Wellness Water could be made by a number of artisans; one of which we call "Prills." Better said, the alterations were caused by a natural influence that we call Life Force, or YINERGY™, and this energy could be transferred to liquids indefinitely and continually with the support of nature through the right carriers. CWR was much more difficult to make and since it was soon to be a product, it needed to be definable by the convention of science. In the early days, Jim added soluble magnesium compounds, which theoretically had beneficial value and provided the analytical people something to evaluate. Soon it became clear that he was actually duplicating an aspect of sea water. If you removed the salt, sodium chloride, from sea water, it was very similar to what Jim was compounding. Could it be that nature was prepared for what was coming? Could it be the restorative potential that the world so desperately needed was stored in the oceans? Why didn't everyone who swam in the ocean receive these beneficial properties?

To make a long story short, Jim believes that nature was prepared, and that all that had to be added to the equation was the knowledge of the energy that animates life, or Life Force. Why did Jim receive this knowledge? Was he special? Actually I don't think so. I think he was just desperately seeking and isn't it said that "if you seek you will find."

Our oceans were full, actually about six ounces in every gallon of sea water, of the most wonderful restorative compound. This compound was mostly a form of water, and since we are mostly water, water very similar to sea water, this seemed to make sense. This compound came with substances to analyze and they were among the most beneficial and least offensive compounds known to man. Our oceans were also full of all the waste of man. We had used them for septic tanks for centuries and even the thought of this offended me. Jim could supersaturate any sea water with the energy of the stone and make it work, but wasn't there a better, a more pristine source? If Jim was going to go to all of the trouble to produce "the most remarkable substance in the world" couldn't he find a source that hadn't seen the foot print of man? And when I use man, I mean the male! Hopefully, most women are too smart to contaminate their home.

Considering that the entire world was at one time or another covered by the ocean and considering that the moisture of CWW is truly unique and that it does not evaporate in the same manner as common water, wasn't it possible to produce something truly wonderful, from sources that were actually and naturally clean?

The answer was yes, and this is why we now use the terms "Ancient Ocean" or "essential oil of sea water" in connection with CWR, or Magic Oil. For now we will leave the details of this source undefined, but we can tell you that there are magnificent, and pristine reserves of very regenerative and restorative substances that science is just now coming to know.

Here is how we describe what CWR or Magic Oil can do: There are two issues in the restoration or maintenance of a living cell, the cell membrane and the fluid that fills it. Both of these materials are principally forms of water. To stay with the simplicity of this presentation, we will simply say that water comes in many different thickness and to be a bit more complex will say that thickness is an aspect of science and probably should not be confused with viscosity, another aspect of science. There are many things that change the viscosity of water, some are called surfactants and alterations in viscosity have much to do with surface tension, while alteration in thickness are generally seen as the product of filling a solution with something that occupies more space, in this case a unique energy.

The water that makes up the parts of living organisms called fluids or membranes are thick waters, while those that fill cells are much thinner. CWR is a thick substance that seems to be easily utilized by living organisms to produce the more dense part of its being. Going out on a further limb, the calcium in bone is held together by something; cartilage is made of a thick substance, fluids are thicker than waters, and so on. Regardless of the other constituents found in the more dense aspect of living organism, they are considered to be highly composed of water or something similar.

Cell Wellness Restorer is "something similar." CWR may be a truly universal building material and the living organisms may be able to use it to enhance rapid reorganization, loosely called restoration. If you can fortify the skeleton, you will by this act alone improve the strength of the entire system. If you can increase the cartilage, you will improve the flexibility of the entire system. If you can restore the integrity of cells on an individual basis you will improve the elasticity of soft tissue or muscle. If the little balls called cells have strong membranes and are perfectly inflated, you will improve their ability to handle the energies that are compatible with it and to repel those that are destructive.

We consider CWR or Magic Oil, or YINERGY™ Oil to be a supplement, as we continually replace the waters of our "living organism" just as we think we do with vitamins and minerals. We believe that CWR is part of the truth and perhaps the missing link in a very serious aspect of maintaining well being. We believe that this liquid is as necessary as water and stand on this necessity.

Almost everyone who has used CWR, and has been evaluated according to good scientific procedure has shown remarkable improvement in well being. The rule of thumb appears to be that if you are not getting the results you wish, if you use more you will. If you treat this simple substance as you would a friend, you will soon find that you truly have one, and that this friend will support you in your quest for life.

THE FOUNTAIN OF YOUTH

If you have the Prills, then you have a piece of Jim's technology and the ability to make your own thin water. The thick water or as we call it the Oil takes far longer to make and this technology is not something that you could use at home.

The objective of these two items is to provide you with replenishment for the forms of water that compose most of your body, with the express intent of aiding in your regeneration into the state of life that is known as youth. There is no precedent for growing younger. In fact this concept is forbidden by the statements such as "if people did not die, our world would soon be over-populated, resulting in insufficient resources and ending in death for us all." "The two immutable truths are death and taxes," and a hundred more. All we can say is that if you have accepted your mortality, if you are planning to grow old and die, then these products should not be incorporated into your life, as they may seriously interfere with your graceful aging and demise.

We cannot yet tell you that using these products will stop the biological clock; only time will tell this After years of watching people become visibly and structurally younger, after hearing them tell us that their pains had gone away and their vitality has returned, after running numerous tests that show alterations in the blood chemistry that could not be attributed to any other reason or cause, we are sure that the use of Thin and Thick Water will improve the quality of life for almost anyone who chooses to bring them into their lives. Will we live forever? Well it is said that we do anyway, so we believe that it makes perfect sense to attempt to make the quality of this part of our lives as high as possible, and this is what this is all about.

If you are reading this, then you either have Thin or Thick Water or both, or you are getting ready to make the choice to get them or forget them. In the following words, we are going to offer a couple of analogies that may ring a bell with some, and some tips that have developed from our experiences and from those of others who have been using the materials over the last few years. The magic in these substances is real: it can be and has been demonstrated under good scientific criteria. Even more, we challenge everyone to be part of the proof. If you would like to have scientific proof and you are willing to pay for this evidence, you can demonstrate an increase in DHEA and magnesium. That story will unfold later.

There are two stories, two analogies that I like to use. The first is that of a brick building and it is very simple and to the point: Building materials are specific to the structure. If you build a brick building, as the bricks fall because of age, you replace them with new bricks and good mortar; such a building will last a thousand years; there are such structures in our world today. If on the other hand, you don't have new bricks and proper mortar, temporary repairs can be effected by filling the holes with mud or plastic, but the building will degrade and eventually fail. A building is specific to the materials of its structure, brick buildings are not totally composed of brick and mortar, but this is the main part of their matrix. Living organisms are not totally composed of water but water, or forms of it, obviously are the single largest constituent. It is our position that the Thick Water is the appropriate form to replace the moisture that the body uses in the formation of thicker materials, cell membrane, cartilage, and to hold the calcium and magnesium in bone. Thin water is the appropriate material to fill these cells, whether these cells be part of soft or hard tissue. These appear to be primary building blocks of living systems, the bricks and the mortar if you like, of life. The proof of these words will only be known by your own personal experience, and a good healthy skeptical logic should move you to have this experience.

Living organisms are extremely similar to rechargeable batteries, and there are constants in such batteries that have been accepted as laws, Galvanic Laws, for a very long time. The best example is the battery of your automobile, but all rechargeable batteries work in the same fashion. There are five constants and if these constants are abridged, the battery will soon fail.

All rechargeable batteries have:

1. A case: in the car a battery and a skin in the human.

2. A grid work: the lead plates in the car battery and the skeleton of a human.

3. An electrolyte: sulfuric acid and water in a car battery and types of water, Thin and Thick Water, and magnesium, in a human.

4. A specific type of energy: say six or twelve volt direct current in the car battery and Life Force in a human.

5. Probably the most important aspect in either case is "flow regulation" or voltage regulation as it is generally called. So a voltage regulator in the lead/acid battery and the primal brain or Medulla Oblongata of the human.

Very simply either system, if it is maintained at peak operating efficiency will last a very long time, theoretically forever. If on the other hand, a galvanic system or rechargeable battery is not maintained, it is destined eventually to fail. That these systems are specific to their design is obvious to anyone who understands galvanic law. That the human version must be governed by this law should also be obvious. As far as we can see, the mystery of life, is simply a matter of our failure to recognize the specifics of the system that we live with, or die from.

The fact that we do not know the design of the human battery appears to be responsible for the "mystery of life" and since life is a mystery, and a mystery by its own nature is simply "something that is unknown" developing the understanding that resolves the mystery may lead to a dynamic alteration in the potential and future of mankind. This new science may also provide an understanding of the issues that are damaging our lives and our environment and perhaps even lead to reconciliation of such issues. This would seriously alter the future, especially of our heirs.

SUMMARY OF WALTRIP'S PATENTS

U. S. Patent Number 4,130,483, December 19, 1978. In accordance with the present invention, a high sulphur content coal is ground into particles and undergoes a coking operation in the presence of steam to form a particulate coke product and a gaseous product including sulphur dioxide and steam. The particulate coke is charged into two settling tanks to form filter beds therein. The aqueous sewage to be treated is introduced into one of the settling tanks for passage through the filter bed within which it reacts with the particulate coke both physically and chemically. A liquid effluent is withdrawn from the bottom of the settling tank while a settled solid product is periodically removed to deplete the filter bed requiring periodic recharging of the settling tank. The liquid effluent is conducted into the second settling tank for passage through the filter bed therein. The gaseous product from the coking operation is passed through a condenser and the condensate conducted to the second settling tank. An electric field is established in the second settling tank in order to electrically charge the particular coke bed. As a result of the foregoing conditions within the second filter tank, the filter bed is operative to remove from the liquid effluent nitrates, phosphates and other such pollutants as well as bacterial contaminants. A liquid product in the form of potable water is accordingly extracted from the bottom of the second settling tank, suitable for irrigation purposes.

U. S. Patent Number 4,214,046, July 22, 1980. Coal converted to coke and ground into particular form, is mixed with an aqua regia solution resulting in a slurry from which solid matter settles out and volatiles are withdrawn. The pH value of the aqua regia solution is so modified by dilution to control reactions within the flurry resulting in a liquid phase that is suitable as a battery electrolyte.

CHAPTER 2

WATER WATER EVERYWHERE AND
NOT A DROP TO DRINK

From a scientific point of view, the most essential factor for human life is air; the second most essential is water. We can live without air for approximately three minutes. Depending upon the temperature, we can live without water for approximately two weeks. The human body is composed of a minimum of 70% water and essentially every living process requires water for the chemical events essential to life. We maintain our normal body temperature through water. We carry waste products out of the body through water. For the last hundred years, physicians have recommended that the average adult consume about two quarts of water per day. Now it is interesting, we should be basing that upon body weight and let us assume that a 150 lb. individual needs two quarts of water and even a baby weighing under ten pounds will consume about a pint and a half of water a day largely through milk. But what about the quality of water? West of Missouri, almost all water is relatively "soft" with alkali in it. East of the Missouri/Kansas line, almost all water is "hard" containing calcium and magnesium. It is well known that deaths from heart disease are lower in areas where the drinking water is hard. Artificially softened water, which is often used in the hard water areas, is extremely unsafe as it usually replaces the calcium and magnesium with sodium and may replace zinc in the pipelines with cadmium. More importantly, over the last 75 years the vast majority of municipal water has been chlorinated and fluoridated. There is increasing evidence that chlorine may be more harmful than sodium. Certainly we do not need extra chlorine in our bodies. Furthermore, the chlorine interferes with absorption of iodine which in my opinion is partly responsible for the widespread, relatively common, subclinical hypothyroidism. One of the other problems with chlorination of water is that if there is any contamination of the municipal water with any by-products of sewage, the chlorine may convert these into carcinogenic agents. About every ten years, a little blurb gets out into the national media about the fact that chlorinated water contains carcinogens. There is no way for city water to be provided safely without chlorination because the chlorination is specifically to kill those bacteria which come from sewage contamination! In other words, we have to chlorinate the water to keep it from killing you from a bacterial infection and somehow we have got to get rid of the chlorine to make it truly healthy.

Even more worrisome is that for the last 60 years most cities have fluoridated their water. There is increasing evidence the fluoride is particularly harmful to bones when used over a lifetime and may well aggravate osteoporosis and cause more brittle bones. Distilled water has no minerals in it and drinking two quarts of that a day could be harmful to your health by leeching some of the normal minerals from your body. The best source of water is spring water or ground water that has been carefully tested to be certain that it has not been contaminated with petrochemicals or bacteria. Those lucky individuals who have access to their own well and ground water should have the water tested for petrochemical contamination at least every three to five

years. The place to do that is the Water Test
Corporation, P. O. Box 6360, Manchester, NH 03108-
6360, phone 1-800-426-8378. The local health
department will analyze the water for bacterial
contamination.

DEHYDRATION AS THE CAUSE OF ILLNESS

In 1992, F. Batmanghelidj, M.D.published one of
the more interesting medical physician commentaries on
water, YOUR BODY'S MANY CRIES FOR WATER,
(Global Health Solutions, Inc., P. O. Box 3189, Falls
Church, VA 22043). Dr. Batmanghelidj says
unequivocally: "It is chronic dehydration that is the root
cause of many of the diseases we confront in medicine at
the present!" Dr. Batmanghelidj believes that there is no
substitute for water and that includes tea, coffee, alcohol,
juice, and any other manufactured beverage. Among
other medical problems, he says that he has treated over
3,000 peptic ulcer sufferers with water alone. He
believes that "dry mouth" is a symptom only at the "end
stages" of dehydration and this dehydration he believes is
responsible for dyspepsia or heart burn, rheumatoid pain,
back pain, anginal pain, headache, leg pain, and indeed,

most illnesses. He reports a young man in his 20's who came to see him one evening in excruciating pain. The patient had taken Cimetidine 300 mg., as well as a full bottle of antacids which had not relieved his pain. Dr. Batmanghelidj prescribed one pint of water, fifteen minutes later one half pint of water, and within twenty minutes, the pain had totally disappeared. Dr. Batmanghelidj believes that in less severe cases, simple water will relieve gastric duodenal pain totally within eight minutes. He goes further to say that pain of colitis or colon pain or "false appendicitis pain" are also equally relieved by adequate intake of water.

Although one might easily understand that water would dilute the excess acid, one of the foundations for gastric pain, it is perhaps more difficult to see how this could affect many other diseases. Dr. Batmanghelidj feels that simple, essential hypertension is a "gross body water deficiency signal." We know that in hypertension the peripheral blood vessels constrict. Dr. Batmanghelidj believes that the constriction is due to a loss of blood volume. He currently makes the very wise statement that water is the best diuretic! Moving beyond this, he feels that high blood cholesterol is the result of the body protecting itself with the cholesterol becoming something of a sludge to prevent the cells from becoming further dehydrated. When one drinks adequate water, the cholesterol will not be needed to protect against dehydration and will go down.

In relation to rheumatoid arthritis, he has a rather interesting argument that the actively growing blood cells in bone marrow take priority over cartilage for available water. If one is relatively dehydrated, then the bone marrow gets the fluid and the cartilage suffers. He, thus, believes that joint pain is due to dehydration of the cartilage and subsequent inflammation.

Moving beyond rheumatoid arthritis, he feels that even allergies and asthma are symptoms of dehydration. His argument is that when one is dehydrated, more histamine is produced to cause constriction of the bronchial muscle so that one will lose less water through the lungs. As one becomes more and more dehydrated, more histamine is produced. He states that with adequate water intake, histamine production will decrease over a period of three to four weeks and bring the unique

50

symptoms of allergies and asthma under control.

Dr. Batmanghelidj argues that anxiety and depression are the results of water deficiency. Water is necessary for the chemical production of electricity in our brain. When we are relatively dehydrated, the level of energy generation is decreased. When there is inadequate energy production, then we become depressed or irritable, which means anxious.

He argues that diabetes is the end result of "brain water deficiency."

Migraine headaches affect some 17% of women and 9% of men in this country. He believes that migraine headaches are brought about by dehydration. He states "the most prudent way of dealing with migraine is its prevention by the regular intake of water."

Now let us go to one of the biggest diseases in America, obesity. Dr. Batmanghelidj quotes two individuals who lost between 30 and 45 lbs. of weight and another who lost 58 lbs. of weight only by drinking water. He always recommends drinking a full glass of water 30 minutes before a meal and at least a minimum of that much two and one half hours after a meal and so as not to "short-change the body," two more glasses of water "around the heaviest meal or before going to bed" - a total of 8 glasses, 8 oz. each daily.

Dr. Batmanghelidj makes some very important observations that mainly if we eat food when we are dehydrated, the concentrated digestive products "draw water" from the cells.

Obviously some very simple and excellent research needs to be done to determine whether Dr. Batmanghelidj's concepts are correct. If they are, it appears as if we could solve a minimum of half of America's medical problems just by having people drink two quarts of water a day. But remember, it must be water and not coffee, tea, juice, or alcohol and as I will emphasize as we proceed with this book, it appears to me at this point in time that this special water which one can produce through the YINERGY™ approach will be by far the healthiest of all water.

Drunvalo Melchizedek states that there are over 200 types of ice and he further states that the outer electrons are complete in the molecules of water found in rivers or lakes and quotes the University of Georgia as having found that all diseased cells are surrounded by "unstructured" water. Unstructured water is defined as missing one electron from its outer orbit and structured water as having no missing electrons, at least in this particular definition. He believes that when water moves through pipes it moves in a spiral way that removes outer electrons creating unstructured water. He thus believes that all water moved through pressurized pipes is associated with disease and states that if we sit in a tub of water we absorb in twenty minutes, up to sixteen ounces of that water. He states that there is an ionized water, SIW, (Super Ionized Water) which has three extra electrons in the water molecule's outer orbits but that it is stable and that if you take the plug of an ordinary lamp and put it into a glass of SIW, it will light the lamp brighter than if plugged into the wall. He states that at a Washington, DC meeting of a "leading environmental research company," a large sample of polluted water that looked and smelled foul was brought in. He demonstrated by placing a small amount of SIW on top of water; over a two hour period it slowly turned the water into what looked like crystal clear distilled water.

He further states that two ounces of automobile oil was poured into a beaker and then a small amount of SIW was poured into the beaker and shaken. In three seconds the oil had disappeared and there were amino acids and proteins which can be used as fertilizer. He believes that 70% to 80% of all the world's hydrocarbon pollution could be cleaned in a very short time with SIW. He states that this SIW water will actually put out even more than gasoline fires. He does not recommend drinking SIW. EXCERPT FROM: "Water - The Source of Life" by Drunvalo Melchizedek, Copyrighted July 1999 by Clear Light. Available on the Internet at: http://www.drunvalo.net/livingwater.html.

In the late 1800's and actually until the 1940's, healing springs all over the world reached perhaps their highest use. Medical professionals of the area were all great proponents. In 1870 Dr. Tyrell, a well known physician at the time, wrote a major volume showing that water was used to cure "all disease," THE ROYAL ROAD TO HEALTH. And just as Dr. Batmanghelidj, he had one chapter entitled "The Cure for All Disease."

In Excelsior Springs, Missouri there are a number

of different springs. Some produce carbonated waters which are ferro-manganese which are believed to increase hemoglobin, temperature, pulse, and weight. They also increase appetite and reduce intestinal activity.

The sulphato-carbonate waters are rich in calcium bicarbonate and are especially indicated in obstinate chronic diarrhea. Uric acid, gravel and calculi are also disintegrated and eliminated by the free use of this class of water.

Chloro-carbonate waters, better known as soda wells, are heavily charged with sodium chloride and bicarbonate combination. They are said to increase the action of the skin when applied externally and by absorption act as a tonic internally to correct acidity, increase the flow of gastric juice, improve appetite, increase the flow of urine and excretion of urea and to prevent putrefactive changes in the intestines.

Chloride waters are said to carry the highest percentage of sodium chloride recorded in any of the Excelsior Spring waters. They act as purgatives.

The sulphato-chloride waters are especially indicated in catarrhal conditions of the mucous membranes of the stomach, intestines, and biliary passages, as well as the urinary tract. They increase the flow of urine and the excretion of uric acid. In large quantities they act as purgatives.

There are actually sixteen separate wells or springs in the Excelsior Springs area with water coming from as shallow as 10 feet and as deep as 1,460 feet. This information is taken from the Bureau of Geology and Mines from Rolla, Missouri, 1919, "Classification of Mineral Waters at Excelsior Springs, Missouri."

Information on the St. Moritz, Switzerland health spa: It is at an altitude of 1800 m above sea-level in a broad valley opening up towards the south-west. It is a strongly stimulating alpine climate with dry air and low in allergens. The mineral sources at St. Moritz are considered the strongest iron sources with carbonic acid in Europe and it is said that mineral baths lead to a strong dilatation of blood-vessels and thus an intensification of blood circulation, reduction of high blood pressure and have a general vivifying and refreshing effect. They believe that it is useful for high blood pressure, poor circulation, after effects of myocardial infarction, etc.

The chalybeate water of the mineral source contains many "precious tracer elements." It is said that its mineral water stimulates digestion, kidney activity, and hematopoiesis. They use peat baths and packs which are said to be useful for treating chronic degenerative and inflammatory diseases, rheumatic disease, peritonitis, menstrual troubles, and stimulating the adrenals and ovaries. It is said that it increases estrogen in the blood.

Perhaps the best known spas in the world are at Baden Baden in Southern Germany which were used by the Romans 2000 years ago and still attract thousands each year.

WATER AND STRUCTURE

It is interesting that scientific exploration of water really only began in the 1800's. Obviously instinct must have led our most ancient ancestors to have recognized the necessity of water in maintaining life. Greek philosophers, including Aristotle, felt that it was so important they considered it one of four essential "elements": earth, air, fire and water. The Chinese added a fifth element, metal. In 1781, Priestly synthesized water out of hydrogen and oxygen and Lavoisier and Cavendish succeeded in decomposing liquid water into "ordinary air" (oxygen) and "inflammable air" (hydrogen). It was not until 1891 that Vernon postulated the aggregation of water molecules to account for the phenomenon of density. From that time forward, it was known that water seemed to be somewhat of an anomaly. In the 1930's, x-ray and infrared studies on water began and soon after the concept of solute molecules in the water were considered the origin for icebergs. And it was only then in the 1950's that significant physicochemical studies of water and its interactions with solutes gradually became popular. Following that it was discovered that the confirmation of proteins was dependent upon water. The structure of hydrogen bonding in water and whether it can bend or disassociate has been one of the major aspects of the physics of water. And it is well known now that all water normally contains a very unusual form called deuterium.

Water has several extremely unique characteristics including an exceptional ability to store heat. "If one mile of water flows from a region of high temperature to a distant region where the temperature is 20 C degrees lower, then the heat transfer amounts to 4.6×10^{13} kcal, which is equivalent to the heat produced by 7 million tons of coal. If a current 100 miles wide and 1/4 mile deep flows at a rate of 1 mph, then 25 miles of water are transported every hour, and the heat energy thus transferred to the cooler region is equivalent to that produced by 175 million tons of coal. All the coal mined in the world in one year would supply heat at this rate for only 12 hours." (From: WATER: A COMPREHENSIVE TREATISE, edited by Felix Franks, Volume 1, Plenum Press, New York-London 1972, page 19) Another oddity of water is that its density is maximum just above the freezing point and this results in higher density at the surface, freezing from the top downward. This is very important for if oceans in the cooler regions of the earth froze from the bottom up, only the surface would thaw in the summer.

Water is also moderately compressible at ordinary temperatures and pressure. And if it were not so compressible, the level of the sea would be 40 meters higher than it is now. Although water is not the only element that expands upon freezing, while most contract, this is one of its chief features. Because it has a very high surface tension, water easily penetrates into small crevices in rocks where upon freezing and expanding, it fragments the rock and breaks it apart into smaller pieces ultimately creating soil. Nearly all chemicals will dissolve in water to a slight extent. Water is more reactive than most other solvents, readily interacting with ions and molecules. It is one of the most corrosive substances known. Some slight radioactive hydrogen occurs in rain and snow. That radioactivity has a half life of 12.5 years so water can be dated by its tritium content. Some of these unusual properties of water and its extremely unique relationship to light remain something of an enigma to most people. Although there are several double-blind excellent scientific studies demonstrating that homeopathic preparations have physiological effects in human beings, there is no chemical or physics explanation that allows for this. In conventional homeopathic preparations, the original substance is diluted up to billions or trillions of times so that according to the laws of physics, no atom of the original substance is still there and yet the "energy" from these atoms seems to have been transferred somehow into the water. After exploring some of the unusual aspects of Jim Carter's thin and thick water substances, I cannot help but wonder whether the laminar crystal increases the possibility of concentrating energy homeopathically.

Water has been known for over 100 years to have unusual physicochemical properties but it was in the 1930's with the introduction of spectrographic techniques that anomalous properties began to be understood and in the 1950's, the key role of the hydrogen bonds between individual water molecules became clear. The two most interesting unusual aspects of water are that each water molecule can bond its hydrogen molecules with four neighboring molecules forming a three dimensional structure, essentially a "crystal." In addition, water has an unusually high capacity to store heat. Hydrogen bonding is often measured by infrared spectroscopy. When the hydrogen bonds are weakened, the water becomes more structured. When water passes into the ice stage, it is coordinated with the four neighbors forming a regular hexagonal structure closely resembling a diamond (another crystal). Because of its ability to structure hydrogen bonding in several ways, there are nine different types of structuring possible. This changing of the hydrogen bonding makes water act to some extent very much like a crystal. In living systems, water is naturally structured around the surface of cell membranes but most of the water has decreased hydrogen bonding resulting in a more random distribution. Water that has been biologically structured has a change in the dielectric constant and its conductivity and can change more easily into unstructured water. Apparently protons can travel between the two types of water via the hydrogen bonds.

Water can store not only thermal energy but also ultraviolet energy. Certain additives such as sugar and polyols also structure water, the ultimate structure being the form water was in prior to the addition of these additives. Interestingly, enzyme activity appears less related to chemical structure of additives than to the ability of the additives to structure water and enzymes appear to "remember" the structured water even after many dilutions. This may be a principle involved in homeopathy where water has been exposed to a specific chemical and then remarkably diluted and yet seems to have a "memory" of the original substance. This ability of water to store memory of chemical structure is believed to be responsible for differing biological effects. Dr. Glen Rein has hypothesized that water cannot only store chemical memories but also frequency memories associated with electromagnetic fields. This concept of structuring water in this way is called imprinting, potenizing, or charging water. It has been stated that homeopathic remedies which are just exposed to electromagnetic fields of different frequencies produce different biological effects and some people believe that traditional homeopathic remedies produced chemically can be made more effective when the water was previously charged with EMF frequency. Rein quotes some authors as feeling that water which has been charged with 10kHz spike wave by direct electrode insertion into the water produces more potent remedies; and in England, Smith at the University of Salford has determined that individuals who are extremely sensitive to electromagnetic waves such as fluorescent lights were known to respond to specific electromagnetic frequencies when they were transferred into water.

Structuring of water by Spiritual healers has also been extensively researched. Olga Worrall, America's most researched healer, and several others, statistically altered infrared absorption of water. This change is considered to be due to physical alterations of hydrogen bonding. While not exactly the same as structured water produced in other ways, such as with magnets or high frequency electromagnetic fields, the "imprinting" of water by the mental/physical energy of a healer has additional implications. Is it the same as Holy Water produced by a priest's blessing? Olga's water and that of other healers has been demonstrated to increase growth of plants. This particular aspect, increased plant growth, is also seen with the use of "Magic Water."

A Czechoslovakian researcher, Patrovskky, observed that water charged with frequencies of less than 500 Hz or in the GHz range (billions per second) affects calcium carbonate solubility. He reported that water charged with those specific frequencies, which he called resonant water, had no effect on plant growth but water charged with electrostatic fields, especially DC magnetic or ultrasound waves, which he called polarized water, stimulated plant growth and had no effect on calcium solubility or infrared spectroscopy.

Magnetically charged water has also been used in Eastern Europe and China where it is thought to help with dissolving lime deposits, desalting soil, accelerating plant growth and to be useful in the treatment of kidney stones.

In his study reported in 1992 at the International Tesla Society in Colorado Springs, Colorado, "Storage of Non-Hertzian Frequency Information in Water," Glen Rein reported that non-Hertzian energy altered the ultraviolet spectra of water in a frequency specific manner. He felt that non-Hertzian energy was quantitatively and qualitatively different from that produced by more conventional electromagnetic waves.

In 1996 Glen Rein, Ph.D. and William A. Tiller, Ph.D., Professor Emeritus of Material Science at Stanford University, reported "Spectroscopic Evidence for Force-Free and Potential-Free Information Storage in Water" (Proceedings of the International Association of

New Sciences International Symposium on New Energy, Denver 1996). These authors used a solenoid coil wound around 14 inches of polyvinyl tubing in a bifillar manner using 580 turns of double-stranded #27 wire. The wire was then partially separated to generate 4 loose terminals, two at the top and two at the bottom of the coil. A 44 Hz sine wave was generated connected to a stereo amplifier and run through the solenoid coil. The coil was wired both with non-cancelled and cancelled generating resistance values of 11 and 22 ohms. Using 2 ml of commercially available reverse osmosis water, the tubes were then treated with either the cancelled or non-cancelled coil configuration for 1-1/2 hours. The water was then transferred to a quartz cuvette and absorption determined with a spectrophotometer. Each sample was read nine times and averaged. Significant differences were then obtained in the values of the cancelled vs non-cancelled water.

Other scientists have worked on increasing the amount of dissolved oxygen in water and in Oklahoma, a commercially available water called Hunza™ drinking water is reported by the Oklahoma State Department of

Health to comply with their standards and in 1999 at the National Sporting Goods Association Trade Show in Chicago, improved athletic performance was reported when athletes drank super oxygenated water. In 25 distance runners they reported that 83% performed better after drinking this super oxygenated water than they did after a regimen of regular bottled water. Fourteen shaved an average of 31 seconds off their 5 kilometer runs. This was prepared by extracting oxygen from the atmosphere and under pressure forcing it through a special container where it is mixed and infused into the water.

As early as 1947, in the 50th Anniversary Volume Commemorating the American Public Health Association, it was stated "At present the control of stream pollution rests largely in the hands of the states."

State legislation is characterized by a lack of uniformity and a general evidence of lack of appreciation. The scientific and economic principles that underlie the problem of stream control limits jurisdiction of the law, leading to serious pollution capable of working great economic injury.

In the past 53 years there has been a marked increase in ground water pollution.

Water pollution has a long history of disease production. As early as 1815, it was known that polluted water contributed to cholera. Eventually this led to public takeover of water supplies and early in the 20th Century to chlorination of water. Although chlorination prevents water borne infectious diseases, it in no way removes petrochemical pollution. Both chlorination and petrochemicals increase carcinogens in water.

Paramagnetic substances are those that concentrate magnetic lines within themselves. They are attracted to areas of higher magnetic flux.

Diamagnetic substances are the opposite - they are attracted to areas of low magnetic flux. Water is diamagnetic. Oxygen is paramagnetic. Water without oxygen will not support life. Water without small amounts of magnesium and calcium is far less healthy. Interestingly, silica is extremely critical in stabilizing the ability of water to hold an electrical charge. A small quantity of silica and magnesium, especially, allow water to be "structured" to hold oxygen. Crystals, water as a crystal, minerals, structuring of water and imprinting of water all suggest that water is versatile and that polluted water can be cleaned. The Waltrip/Kearns experiments reported by Bob F. and the Waltrip patents all point in this direction. Additionally, the Magic Water and Prill Water introduced by Jim Carter suggest that there are ways to improve the quality of water so that we can enjoy that two quarts of water recommended each day!

CHAPTER 3

HOLY WATER, SACRED OIL

A little common sense and observation would have taught our ancestors many thousands of years ago that water is essential to life. It becomes quite obvious when there is no rain that things don't grow and water has had a magical connotation throughout much of history. Virtually every religion including Christianity and Judaism have used water in some form of sacramental ceremony. In the Catholic Church water is used in the sacrament for Baptism (as it is in all Christian religions), blessing of bells, consecrating a church, the blessing and sacraments carried out with holy water itself.

Water has been used in all the major religions as a "symbol of purification." In Ancient Egypt, the Nile was used for sacred baths. In India, it was and is the Ganges. In Babylonia, it was the Euphrates.

In Judaism, water was used for ritual cleansing. Well before the birth of Christ, converts to Judaism were required to bathe themselves as a sign of entering the covenant and John The Baptist urged Jews to be baptized in the Jordan for remission of sin. John then, of course, baptized Jesus at the beginning of his public ministry. This baptism (Greek baptein-to dip) became the foundation for Christianity. Paul (Romans 6:3-11) considered baptism to be part of the death and resurrection and in the early church, it was considered the beginning of illumination, renunciation of the world, flesh and the devil. By the 3rd Century A.D., preparation for baptism had become a major rite with a preparatory fast, official confession of sins, renunciation of the devil, immersion in water, and then anointing with oil. As the Catholic Church began to split, the practice of Baptism became much more variable and still varies significantly in many Protestant Churches, some using a mere sprinkling of water and others insisting that full immersion is necessary.

Early church history suggests that the concept of Holy Water goes back to at least the year 400 as a tribute to the Apostle St. Matthew. Pope Alexander I lived in the Second Century and is also said to have used water

71

but there is no written documentation of this. In most cases in the Sacrament of Baptism, flowing water such as sea or river water was used. The "Pontifical Scrapion of Thumis," a fourth-century bishop, and the "testamentum Domini," contained information concerning blessing of both oil and water during Mass. In Scrapion's Pontifical the blessing reads: "We bless these creatures in the Name of Jesus Christ, Thy only Son; we invoke upon this water and this oil the Name of Him Who suffered, Who was crucified, Who arose from the dead, and Who sits at the right of the Uncreated. Grant unto these creatures the power to heal; may all fevers, every evil spirit, and all maladies be put to flight by him who either drinks these beverages or is anointed with them, and may they be a remedy in the Name of Jesus Christ, Thy only Son." (The Catholic Encyclopedia: HOLY WATER). There are other mentions of water sanctified by liturgical blessing by individual blessing by some holy person. St. Epiphanius recorded that a man named Joseph poured water on a madman, essentially doing an exorcism and making the sign of the cross. This same Joseph later, even though a layman, was said to have overcome witchcraft using blessed water. Theodoret recorded that the Bishop of Apamea made water sanctified by the sign of the cross and that Aphraates cured an emperor's horse by making it drink water blessed by the sign of the cross. In the sixth century it was said that blessed water was capable of curing quartan fever. In these early days, the faithful believed that Holy Water possessed curative powers and this was particularly true of baptismal water. Baptismal water was always carefully preserved throughout the year and was considered free from corruption because of it having been used in baptism. At times individuals not only kept it in their homes but watered their fields, vineyards, and gardens with such Holy Water.

Early on, some churches kept Holy Water at the entrance to the church and the faithful were sprinkled with it as they entered the church. In the Greek Orthodox Church, apparently Holy Water was made at the beginning of each lunar month. Interestingly, this rite may have been established in order to overcome the pagan feast of the new moon. In the ninth century Pope Leo IV ordered that each priest bless water every Sunday and sprinkle the people with it. Individuals were allowed to carry some of the Holy Water away afterward to sprinkle their houses, fields, vineyards, and cattle. Various churches in different dioceses had variable practices of how or when water was to be blessed but interestingly there are two Sundays when it is not and was not to be blessed; namely Easter Sunday and Pentecost. The reason for that is that water for baptism is blessed and consecrated on the eve of those two feasts.

The concept or ceremony of blessing began in the 8th Century. Paul (Romans 6:4-6) stated that "through baptizing we rise with Christ into the newest of life." In the 9th Century, the practice of sprinkling Holy Water on the face before mass became a ritual in the Frankish realm. It later spread into Italy. In the middle ages, Holy Water began to be sprinkled upon the graves of the dead. Holy Water is ordinary water which has been sanctified by the blessings of a priest. At one time, the blessing involved the addition of salt placed into the water in the form of a ceremony. This particular ceremony came from the incident of the miraculous cure of poisoned water when the prophet Elisha used salt to purify the water of a spring (Kings 2:19-22). In the Roman ritual a priest prays: "May this creature of yours, when used in your ministries and endowed with your grace, serve to cast out demons and to banish disease. May everything that this water sprinkles in the homes and gatherings of the faithful be delivered from all that is unclean and hurtful; let no breath of contagion hover, no taint of corruption; let all the wiles of the lurking enemy come to nothing. By the sprinkling of this water may everything opposed to the safety and peace of the occupants of these homes be banished, so that in calling on your holy name, they may know the well-being they desire, and be protected from every peril; through Christ our Lord. Amen." Those who are in good grace in the church are allowed to take Holy Water home and to sprinkle the sick, homes, and fields, with it. The church recommends that they actually put it in fonts in their homes and use it to bless themselves daily. During the Easter time, Holy Water is distributed to millions of people the world over so that water blessed on Easter Sunday is considered above that blessed on ordinary days. Water is specially blessed and part of many rituals within the church including a specific blessing in honor of the Virgin Mary and St. Torellius. That water is to be drunk by the sick. Water blessed in the name of St. Peter is used either for drinking or sprinkling on those who wish to be delivered from evil spirits, illness or suffering of body or spirit. Water blessed in honor of St. Vincent is used to "heal the sick, strengthen the infirmed, cheer the downcast, purify the unclean, and give full well-being to those who seek it." Water blessed with a relic or image of a Saint falls into these categories. Blessing of the water in the name of St. Raymond has been done "for all who suffer from fever." In blessing of water in honor of St. Alvin, relics of the Saint are immersed in the water and those who drink the water do so with expectation of regaining health. When water is blessed in honor of St. Ignatius or St. Vincent de Paul, the relics are left in the reliquary and a medal is substituted for the relics in the ceremony of blessing the water. In some churches, people may bring water, wine, bread, fruit, etc. to be blessed. The priest then sprinkles these items with Holy Water.

SPRINGS AND BATHS

Lourdes - Lourdes is the best known Holy Spring in the modern world. In 1858, Bernadette Soubirous, a young, poor and uneducated French girl, began having visions of the Virgin Mary. When she had one of these visions, she went into a state of "ecstasy." On February 25, 1858 her fame had grown to the point that many people came to see her. Bernadette was praying at a grotto called Massabielle; she turned from the grotto and started toward the nearby river. She turned back to the grotto and began digging in the dirt. A muddy ooze seeped from the hole and Bernadette attempted to drink it but very quickly very clear water began to trickle from this spot toward the river and the water flows today at a rate of over 30,000 gallons a day. People began to imitate Bernadette and to drink and wash with the water. As sick individuals got well and the injured became cured, the water began to be called miraculous. By 1981 only 65 cases examined at Lourdes were declared by the church to be miraculous but millions of people worldwide have claimed that they have been cured or helped by the water of this spring. The water from the spring has been piped to taps and baths at the grotto and is shipped all over. Lourdes water is not considered Holy Water. It has received no special blessing but the Lourdes Center in Boston, Massachusetts in cooperation with the Archbishop of Boston and the Bishop of Lourdes distribute Lourdes water, organize pilgrimages to Lourdes, etc. Lourdes water is free but a donation to cover the cost of shipping and mailing is requested.

Lourdes in 1858 was a city of about 5,000 inhabitants located along the river Pau at the entrance to the high valleys of the Pyrenees. Today some 4 million visitors pass through Lourdes each year. All French and Belgium dioceses sponsor annual pilgrimages to Lourdes. Each year 650,000 sick individuals are received in three reception centers twice a week and an actual mass is celebrated in honor of St. Pius X. At least twice a week communal anointing of the sick is carried out.

In 1917 visions of the Virgin Mary appeared at Fatima, an area which had no known spring but because pilgrims began to come to this spot, the Bishop of Leiria broke ground to build a cistern to hold rain water for use by the pilgrims. As ground was broken for the event in

1921, a pure spring of drinking water bubbled up in a crystalline stream and this water flows by the monument of the Sacred Heart in the Sanctuary of Fatima at the very spot where the vision of the Virgin Mary appeared to the three peasant girls. This water has also been distributed throughout the world and many miracles have been claimed as a result of use of this water but none of these have been agreed to at this point by the church.

January 6 is considered the day of Baptism of Jesus. On this day, water is blessed preferably at streams, lakes and natural bays, etc., to honor the occasion. In Greece the Aegean Sea, the Adriatic and the Mediterranean are all blessed. In a lengthy service, the cross is actually tossed into the blessed body of water to be retrieved by swimmers who receive a prize for their efforts and this ceremony supplies Holy Water for the coming year. All the homes in the parish are blessed after this feast and again after Easter.

In Russia, holes in the form of crosses are cut into frozen rivers and the blessing is performed over these open areas.

In the Catholic Church there are seven "Great

Sacraments," all associated with blessings and most with Holy Water and/or Oil. The Eucharist is considered a symbol for the concept that all food is holy. All sacraments that involve the sprinkling of water are called the cleansing power of Baptism. Beyond the Eucharist, there is the Baptism of course which is traditionally done by immersion in water but in some Protestant churches only through sprinkling of water.

SACRED OIL

In the Eastern Orthodox Church it is more common to use oils that have been blessed. The highest is the Holy Myron which contains almost 100 ingredients and is blessed on various occasions by patriarchs of different Byzantine jurisdictions. Another kind of Sacred Oil is Prayer Oil blessed each time the anointing of the sick is celebrated by a priest. Sometimes oil that is to be used in a meal is blessed and on occasions, oil is used even from burning lamps. A mixture of oil and fragrances is poured over individuals who have died before they are buried. Next in sacraments to Baptism is Confirmation. Then there is Penance for reconciliation. Each of these involves anointing with use of Holy Oil or

Sacred Oil. Anointing of the Sick or Extreme Unction is based upon the letter of James 5:14-15. "Is anyone among you sick? Let him ask for the presbyters of the church, and let them pray over him, anointing him with oil in the name of the Lord..." The actual official ceremony of the anointing of the sick took place in the 9th Century initially only if one was expected to die but it is sometimes used when patients have serious illnesses thus reviving the concept of possible healing from the anointing process.

In general until 1970, most Holy Oil started with olive oil. After that it was decided that Holy Oils could be made from any plant. The blessing of oils was traditionally done on Holy Thursday by a Bishop at a cathedral and the supply was distributed to local churches. Any that was not used over the coming year was burned in a sanctuary lamp. Holy Oil in the Catholic Church is used in sacraments of Baptism, Confirmation, and Holy Orders (confirmation of a priest), as well as in the sacrament of healing. Actually the oil is used also for blessing tower bells, baptismal water and for consecrating churches, alters, chalices, and patens. Traditionally Holy Oil in the Church was a mixture of olive oil and balsam.

The church also recognizes the use of a lay person in performing a sacrament such as a signing on the forehead with a cross using the oil. This ordinarily would be used for a healing or a protection. Several centuries ago during the English suppression of Catholicism in Ireland, priests had to visit homes secretly where mass could be said at night and this began the tradition of Christmas candles. Parishioners would place candles in their windows to let priests know that they were welcome. The candles came to be considered an invocation of the sacred, not quite like Sacred Oil but still a spiritual ritual.

The concept of Holy Oil in the Catholic Church dates at least to the fourth century as well as is mentioned in the Prayer Book of Serapion. This book contains the formula for the blessing of oil so that individuals were both baptized and confirmed into the church in a single ceremony. But even in the fourth century, there was a separate form of blessing for the oil for the sick, for water, and for bread. It is essentially considered an invocation to Christ to provide power to cure the sick, to purify the soul, to drive away impure spirits, and to wipe out sins.

Of course in the Old Testament, oil was used to consecrate priests and kings, as well as sacrifices, legal purifications, and the consecration of altars. (Exod., XXX, 23,33; XXXIX, 27,29; etc.).

In the early Church the Pope himself made the oil before Mass on Holy Thursday. This same oil also was used later for Extreme Unction. Very large amounts of oil were consecrated at that time. Currently the bishop blesses three different types of oil; one for Baptism, one for the sick in the Sacrament of Extreme Unction, and finally that of the chrism, which is a mixture of olive oil and balsam and used in the administration of the Sacrament of Confirmation.

Even in the early days of the Church, the olive oil that was used in making the Eucharist bread was blessed and oil that was used in numerous lamps throughout the churches was blessed and, when the oil was used to burn in front of a famous tomb or shrine, it was particularly venerated as a relic.

In the early days the Greek word chrisma was used to designate any substance that was involved in anointing but eventually the word chrism was restricted to oil used in specific ceremonies, especially the Sacraments of Baptism and Confirmation. Always there have been two elements in a legitimate chrism, olive oil and balsam. For chrism especially, the blessing must be done by a Bishop and although it is particularly restricted to Baptism, Confirmation and Holy Orders, it is also used in the consecration of churches, chalices, patens, altars and altar-stones, bells, and baptismal water. The chrism is applied to the forehead of a person in the form of a cross after Baptism, the head and hands of a bishop at his consecration, and the hands of a priest at his ordination. The walls of churches are anointed with the same holy oil, and the parts of the sacred vessels used in Mass, as well as the paten and chalice are always blessed with this particular oil. It is felt that oil gives strength and flexibility to the limbs and that balsam preserves whatever it touches from corruption. (Reference for Holy Water and Holy Oil: 1. THE CATHOLIC SOURCE BOOK, edited by Rev. Peter Klein, Brown

ROA Publishing Media, Dubuque, Iowa, ; 2. A
HANDBOOK OF CATHOLIC SACRAMENTALS by
Ann Ball, Our Sunday Visitor Publishing Division,
Huntington, Indiana 46750, 1991.)

In summary, there is a long history of the use of special water and oil for healing and to invoke health.

My use of the term Holy Water, Sacred Oil to describe the unique water and oil discovered by Jim Carter, will qualify, as you will see, because they clearly have health and healing properties.

CHAPTER 4

WEATHER, WATER AND HEALTH

Weather has been known to affect health for at least 2000 years. Hippocrates, the "Father" of medicine, emphasized the importance of climate and seasons on health and disease. And although physicians know the remarkable seasonal and weather variations with some diseases, virtually no attention is paid to the striking effects of weather changes. Migraine is particularly triggered by weather fronts moving in or out. Cerebral aneurysms and even peptic ulcers have a seasonal relationship. Despite modern medicine's failure to pay attention to weather, Hippocrates wrote extensively about weather, especially heat and cold and water:

The following is from Hippocrates with an English translation by W. H. S. Jones, published in London by William Heinemann, Ltd. in 1931, Volume 4, page 129: "All diseases occur at all seasons, but some diseases are more apt to occur and to be aggravated at certain seasons." Page 1125: "It is chiefly the changes

86

of the seasons which produce diseases, and in the seasons the great changes from cold or heat, and so on according to the same rule." Volume 1, published in 1923, page 29: "So also when bad physicians, who comprise the great majority, treat men who are suffering from no serious complaint, so that the greatest blunders would not affect them seriously - such illnesses occur very often being far more common than serious disease - they are not shown up in their true colors to laymen if their errors are confined to such cases; but when they meet with a severe, violent and dangerous illness, then it is that their errors and want of skill are manifest to all." Page 27: "And that physician who makes only small mistakes would win my hearty praise. Perfectly exact truth is but rarely to be seen, for most physicians seem to me to be in the same case as bad pilots;". Page 29: "The mistakes of the latter are unnoticed so long as they are steering in a calm, but, when a great storm overtakes them with a violent gale, all men realize clearly then that it is their ignorance and blundering which have lost the ship. So also, when bad physicians, who comprise the great majority, treat men who are suffering from no serious complaint, etc. etc." Page 43: "And I believe that of all the powers, none hold less sway in the body than cold and heat. My reasons are these. So long as the hot and cold in the body are mixed up together, they cause no pain. For the hot is temperate and moderated by the cold, and the cold by the hot. But when either is entirely separated from the other, then it causes pain."

The following quotation is taken from, THE GENUINE WORKS OF HIPPOCRATES, by Francis Adams, published by William Wood & Co., 1929 New York, Volume 1, Page 156: "Whoever wishes to investigate medicine properly, should proceed thus: In the first place to consider the seasons of the year, and what effects each of them produces (for they are not at all alike, but differ much from themselves in regard to their changes). Then the winds, the hot and the cold, especially such as are common to all countries, and then such as are peculiar to each locality. We must also consider the qualities of the waters, for as they differ from one another in taste and weight, so also do they differ much in their qualities." Page 157, "...and in particular, as the season and the year advances, he can tell what epidemic diseases will attack the city, either in summer or in winter, and what each individual will be in danger of experiencing from the change of regimen. For knowing the changes of the seasons, the rising and setting of the stars, how each of them takes place, he will be able to know beforehand what sort of a year is going to ensue. ....and if it shall be thought that these things belong rather to meteorology, it will be admitted, on second thoughts, that astronomy contributes not a little, but a very great deal, indeed to medicine for with the seasons the digestive organs of men undergo a change."

Modern research reveals that the most definitive aspects of weather are temperature, relative humidity and barometric pressure. All of these affect the relative hydration of the body, or water balance. Rising temperature, falling humidity and falling barometric pressure increase the number of health complaints and symptoms including:

> Fatigue
>
> Bad moods/depression/irritability
>
> Headaches
>
> Restless/disturbed sleep

Poor concentration

Nervousness

Pain

Emergency room visits

Increased mistakes

Forgetfulness

Dizziness

Heart palpitations

Psychotic breaks

Higher blood pressure

Delayed reaction times

Death rate

Suicides

Birth/delivery rates increase

Conception rates decrease

Overall sickness increases

Colds

Asthma

Heart attacks

Glaucoma

Infections

Falling temperature, rising barometric pressure

and rising humidity improve health. About half of healthy people report being weather sensitive and even healthy people who are not aware of being weather sensitive have increased symptoms during the weather risk conditions listed above. More critically, individuals who are already ill or weak have a markedly increased sensitivity to weather changes.

Weather changes are stressors that strongly influence health, illness and death. These weather changes force biorhythms to "high peaks and deep depressions."

Equally ignored but critically important are reactions to drugs. Individuals should carefully monitor themselves and decrease dosages of these drugs during hot weather:

Alcohol

Anticoagulants

Antihypertensives

Anti-Parkinsonian drugs

Antispasmodics

Atropine-like drugs/Belladonna

Cortisone/Prednisone

Neuroleptics

Parasympathomimetics

Phenothiazines

Sedatives

Sleeping pills

Diuretics

All tranquilizers/tricyclic antidepressants

During cold weather the following drugs should be decreased:

Analgesics

Barbiturates

Hallucinogens

Monoamine oxidase inhibitors

Neuroleptics

Narcotics

Tetracyclines

All tranquilizers

How much? Obviously careful attention and medical caution should be foremost but dosages might optimally be decreased 10 to 25% under extreme temperature changes. Alternatively, I believe that those adults who drink at least 2 quarts of YINERGY™ water per day will maintain cell hydration better. And, of course, it seems probable that health of these individuals and their need for drugs will decrease.

IONS

Not too surprisingly the modern research quoted above is the effect of ions in the air, greatly affected by humidity. As early as the 1930's a Swedish engineer, Nils Lindenbald, noted that exposure to positive polarity led to depression; exposure to negative polarity led to striking improvement in mood. Lindenbald and his supervisor, Dr. Clarence Hansell, Chief of the RCA Radio Transmission Lab in Long Island reasoned that there might be a link between the man-made ions and those produced in nature. They also learned that gas flames and electric heaters produced positive ions similar to those produced in this country by the Santa Ana Winds. Their research led to findings that high blood pressure could be treated without drugs by negative ionization of the atmosphere. Asthma was improved in 60% of asthmatics. Students become more drowsy in a closed classroom, probably contributed by both the imbalance of light and the increase in positive ions produced by fluorescent lights. Viruses are repelled by negative ions; attracted to humans by positive ions. When the body becomes positive, viruses "attack" humans more powerfully.

Effects of Positive Ions:

Fatigue

Headache

Dizziness

Nausea

Breathing difficulties

Asthma

Sinusitis

Pain, especially in arthritis

Increased blood pressure and pulse

Slower healing

More infections

Depression

Nervousness

Bad temper

Intolerance

Lack of confidence

Effects of Negative Ions:

Optimism

Exhilaration

Good temper

Confidence

Relief of

hay fever

asthma

sinusitis

Decreased blood pressure and pulse

Faster wound healing

Decreased pain

Decreased growth of transplanted cancer

Now when we look at the effects Jim Carter reports with exposure to his black crystals, gold iodide, we see a strong correlation. The gold iodide "bed" is a strong generator of negative ions!

CHAPTER 5

DHEA - THE HEALTH AND YOUTH HORMONE

DHEA, dehydroepiandrosterone, is the most prevalent and one of the most essential hormones in human health. Of considerable interest is the fact that most other animals do not have significant levels of DHEA. Thus when we see the striking number of illnesses which have low levels of both DHEA and magnesium, a possible connection between these essential chemicals begins to appear. Even a 10% increase in DHEA levels is associated with a 48% decrease in death from cardiovascular disease and a 36% decrease in mortality from all causes. Unfortunately, the majority of Americans lose 80 to 90% of their optimal DHEA between ages 30 and 80.

In fact, it is commonly reported that decreasing DHEA levels are inevitable with aging. But I have seen healthy, active 80 year olds with optimal DHEA levels and I have seen stressed-out 30 year olds with low or deficient levels of DHEA. WITH FEW EXCEPTIONS, low or deficient DHEA is found in every illness. Note the frequent overlap of this discussion with that of magnesium (next chapter). Most critically, DHEA blocks carcinogenesis, retards aging and cardiovascular disease and diabetes and even obesity. Interestingly, USA TODAY on 9/5/96 carried a cover story, "DHEA: Is This Hormone the Fountain of Youth." And THE SCIENCES in its September/October 1995 issue carried an article "Forever Young."

The DHEA story begins with cholesterol, the foundation chemical for brain, nerve tissue and hormones. Of all natural biochemicals, cholesterol is the most essential and most common. It is unfortunate that medicine has maligned this critical and beneficial essence of life chemical. IT IS NOT CHOLESTEROL THAT IS A PROBLEM. It is some metabolic errors and/or stress induced dysfunction that raise cholesterol. In fact, not only can we not live without cholesterol, we make cholesterol even without eating it! Ten minutes of stress will cause the body to produce more cholesterol than you get from an egg. Actually eggs are one of the best of all foods; and the cholesterol in eggs comes with an ideal emulsifier, lecithin. Perhaps the myth of cholesterol is best dispelled by the Colorado man who ate 25 eggs a day and had a cholesterol level of only 125.

In other words, except in the very rare condition of familial hypercholesterolemia, the blood level of cholesterol remains "normal," that is below 200 units except when total stress produces blocks to the usual metabolic pathways in which cholesterol is used to make various healthy homeostatic (balancing) hormones. In general, under stress, testosterone, estrogen and even thyroid hormones decrease while cholesterol increases. Unfortunately, one of the normal stress modulators, DHEA, is also blocked when stress exceeds the body's ability to compensate. One of the significant factors in that normal compensatory mechanism is magnesium. As noted in the next chapter, magnesium is critical in stabilizing cellular membrane charge. Physical inactivity, obesity, anger, anxiety, depression, pollution, electromagnetic excess, and deficiency of any essential nutrient may lead in this way to hypercholesterolemia and DHEA depletion.

DHEA is produced in the adrenal glands in both

men and women; men produce about one-third more than women as they also produce DHEA in the testes. The core of the adrenals, the cortex, produces cortisol, androgens, aldosterone, and small amounts of estrogen. Interestingly aldosterone, a major regulator of water, is regulated significantly by potassium, a primarily intracellular mineral, as is magnesium.

Cholesterol is connected in the adrenal cortex to pregnenolone which can then be converted into progesterone, DHEA and androstenedione, the latter made famous in 1998 by Mark McGwire. For unknown reasons, much of the DHEA is bound to a sulfate molecule, RENDERING IT INACTIVE. DHEA and androstenedione can be converted into testosterone. Progesterone can also be converted into cortisone and aldosterone. Actually only 5% of total male testosterone is derived from adrenal androstenedione; the rest from the testes. On the other hand, two-thirds of female testosterone is derived from adrenal androstenedione, the rest is produced in the ovaries.

The major pathways include:

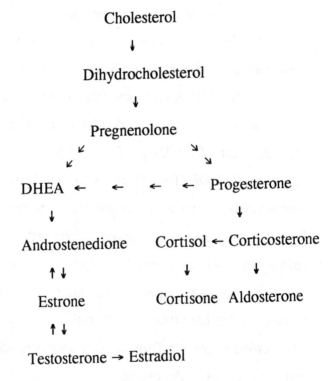

Cholesterol
↓
Dihydrocholesterol
↓
Pregnenolone

DHEA ← ← ← ← Progesterone
↓   ↓
Androstenedione   Cortisol ← Corticosterone
↑↓   ↓   ↓
Estrone   Cortisone Aldosterone
↑↓
Testosterone → Estradiol

In brief summary, DHEA counterbalances the effects of cortisone; inhibits glucose-6-phosphate dehydrogenase important in glucose metabolism; inhibits the pentose shunt and ornithine decarboxylase (perhaps important in growth hormone regulation); blocks the potassium channel (perhaps important in maintaining intracellular magnesium); and inhibits cytokineses which makes it antiinflammatory. It lowers cholesterol and enhances immune function; it is also an antioxidant.

DHEA is a major marker for age and health. Its major effect in a coping person is anti-stress, meaning that the increased cortisone produced by stress is subsequently normally brought back down to baseline by a rise in DHEA. DHEA similarly has antidiabetic action, as cortisol raises blood sugar and either spares or enhances effects of insulin. DHEA protects against both immune and autoimmune diseases; it enhances immune function protecting against infections, especially viral ones, as well as protecting against cancer. It has significant anti-obesity effects, perhaps related to its down-regulation of the stress response.

Interestingly high animal fat diets and obesity lead

to low levels of DHEA. Additionally DHEA is intimately related to thyroid function; primary thyroid disease, especially low thyroid production, leads to low DHEA levels.

Low levels of DHEA are found in women up to nine years BEFORE development of breast cancer. And in my experience, men may have low DHEA levels for four or more years prior to development of prostate cancer.

Insulin, blood sugar and cortisone all cause increased secretion of DHEA into urine and prolonged stress, which may raise insulin, blood sugar and cortisol, eventually leads to low DHEA blood levels.

Many clinical studies of DHEA are suspect as most laboratories are notoriously inaccurate. In testing six labs where we sent three samples of the same blood on up to ten patients, only one lab was accurate. That is, most labs, for the same blood, gave values 50 to 300% different! Only Nichols Labs, now Quest Diagnostics of Capistrano, California, has an accuracy of 1 to 5%. DHEA sulfate levels may be more accurate but at least four separate reports suggest that DHEA-S is not clinically as useful as DHEA. For instance, ACTH ordinarily increases DHEA but not necessarily DHEA-S. Similarly in 108 seropositive HIV men with low CD4 lymphocytes, DHEA was predictive of disease progression but DHEA-S was not.

Low levels of DHEA have been reported in AIDS, Alzheimers, many types of cancer, coronary artery disease, depression, diabetes, hypertension, lupus erythematosus, multiple sclerosis, pemphigus, psoriasis, rheumatoid arthritis, and viral infections. Indeed the only illnesses in which DHEA may be normal are schizophrenia and early in alcoholism and panic attacks.

In evaluating DHEA levels in several thousand patients, I have come to the conclusion that DHEA is the major reflector of stress reserves or overall health.

DHEA LEVELS AND STRESS

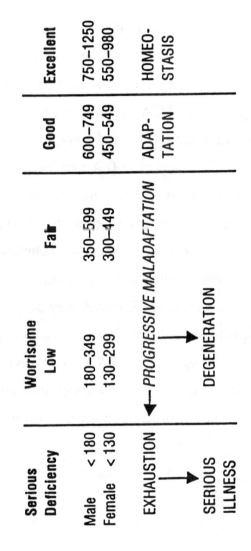

	Serious Deficiency	Worrisome Low	Fair	Good	Excellent
Male	< 180	180–349	350–599	600–749	750–1250
Female	< 130	130–299	300–449	450–549	550–980
	EXHAUSTION	*PROGRESSIVE MALADAFTATION*		ADAP-TATION	HOMEO-STASIS
	SERIOUS ILLNESS	DEGENERATION			

About 50% of all patients seen at our clinic have levels in the poor to fair level and the other 50% are clearly deficient! And even in several hundred non-patients, students attending our seminars, a majority are low or clearly deficient.

It is likely that six hours or more of airplane travel is at least temporarily depleting of DHEA. One otherwise healthy young woman had a DHEA level of only 180 ng/dL two days after flying to the United States from Australia. Twelve days later it had rebounded to 560 ng/dL.

When I first became interested in DHEA ten years ago, I intuited that perhaps one reason for DHEA deficiency was a block in making progesterone which decreases so dramatically at menopause. Thus, I initially recruited seven men with low DHEA levels and had them use natural progesterone cream 1/4 teaspoon twice a day. At six weeks, DHEA levels had increased in six of seven men. By twelve weeks this increase in DHEA had stabilized at 30 to 100% above baseline. Most men also reported becoming more horny! When I published this material, a French professor of endocrinology wrote that there is no known pathway for progesterone to be converted to DHEA! Fortunately hundreds of my patients do not know there is no pathway so they have usually responded with significant increases in DHEA with the use of progesterone cream. Indeed, I have a patent on this process, Patent Number 5,609,617.

Continuing to seek safe ways of RESTORING DHEA, I next suspected that stimulating twelve specific acupuncture points I call the Ring of Fire would raise DHEA. The points are:

Bilateral Kidney (K3) - the hollow inside each ankle.

Conception Vessel 1 (CV 1) - the hollow in the center of the perineum, or Conception Vessel 2 (CV 2) - the top of the genitals, center of pubic bone. Conception Vessel 6 (CV 6) - about 1-1/2 cm. below the umbilicus.

Bladder 22 (B 22) - 2 cm lateral to the spinous process at the junction of the second and third lumbar vertebrae.

Conception Vessel 18 (CV 18) - 1-1/2 cm. below the sternal notch.

Bilateral Master of the Heart (MH 6) - the sympathetic control point, 2 cm. above the wrist, on anterior forearm in center.

Bilateral Large Intestine (LI 18) - window of the sky, located 1 cm. below the mastoid between the sternocleidomastoid and trapezius muscles.

Governing Vessel 20 (GV 20) - at the center top of the head above the top of the ears.

Again DHEA increased 30 to 100% with either of two stimulators, the Liss TENS or GigaTENS. And I received a patent for this process, Patent Number 5,609,617.

Next, I suspected that a chronic deficiency of organic sulfur could lead to DHEA depletion. When I gave 1 gm/day of MSM, methylsulphonylmethane, five of ten individuals had increases in DHEA. Looking for a co-factor, I asked the ten whether they were taking Vitamin C, since the adrenal glands have the highest concentration of Vitamin C of any organ. Only those who were already taking Vitamin C had an increase in DHEA. When we added Vitamin C to MSM in those who originally failed to respond, we found an increase of

50 to 100% in DHEA. After one month, we then added beta 1,3 glucan, a major immune enhancer and the active ingredient in Sacred Mushroom Tea and observed a further increase in DHEA. The formula, Patent Number 5,891,853, is my Youth Formula and a daily supply contains:

    2 grams Vitamin C

    1 gram MSM

    6 mg. Beta 1,3 glucan

Interestingly, although these three widely varied techniques each increase DHEA, they are also synergistic. That is all three together:

    YINERGY™ Eugesterone™

    Ring of Fire Stimulation

    YINERGY™ Youth Formula

raise DHEA better than any one approach and together they increase DHEA 100 to 300%!

Then, two years ago I met Jim Carter and was introduced to his concepts of Magic Oil, Magic Water, and the Star Chamber. I talked with Rochelle and a number of others who had glowing tales of their rejuvenation or "cures" with use of these unusual materials. I also experienced the Star Chamber twice. I felt totally energized with decreased appetite for two days. I reasoned that anything so amazing must raise DHEA.

A week later I had 32 of my students volunteer to use 2 oz. of the oil in a bath, soaking for 20 to 30 minutes daily for three months. Much to my surprise, all but two of them experienced a DROP in DHEA!

Going the next step, I suggested to 20 individuals who were overweight that they do the soak baths with 8 oz. of oil. Results were again disappointing. Convinced that the "right amount" of oil would raise DHEA we enlisted 20 people to do the soaks in a bath with 16 oz. of oil.

Hooray! After only four weeks, DHEA levels came up significantly.

On a follow up visit to see Jim, I suddenly thought that perhaps the secret was the 25% magnesium content of the oil. Our next experiment was to have 16 people with low magnesium soak the feet 20 minutes and to spray the skin with a 50/50 mixture of oil and water. Eureka! The intracellular magnesium came up.

NOW I HAD THE CONNECTIONS: THE
RIGHT AMOUNT OF MAGIC OIL COULD
NORMALIZE INTRACELLULAR MAGNESIUM AND
DHEA!

So what is my recommendation to the average person: EVERYONE can benefit from the use of YINERGY™ oil. If you feel healthy and have no known illnesses, my personal recommendations are:

*Take YINERGY™ Essentials 2 to 4 per day. This is the best multivitamin-mineral combination I know.

* Take YINERGY™ Youth Formula 2 twice a day. This helps optimize DHEA.

* Use YINERGY™ Oil daily

*Soak in bath containing 2 to 8 oz. or

*Soak your feet in it or

*Spray the 50/50 mixture on your body once or twice daily.

Note a small percentage of people get some irritation of sensitive skin (feet, scrotum, vulva, face, etc.) If any irritation occurs, dilute this oil further.

FOR ANYONE with ANY illness or symptoms (See Magnesium Chapter).

* Find a physician who will check your intracellular magnesium level ONLY THROUGH Intracellular Diagnostics, 553 Pilgrim Drive, Suite B, Commerce Park, Foster City, CA 94404, (800) 874-4804.

and

DHEA level ONLY THROUGH Quest Diagnostics of Capistrano, CA (800) 225-7483.

For men, if DHEA is above 180 but below 750 (it will be if you have any illness or significant stress) or for women, if DHEA is above 130 but below 550 (it will be if you have any illness or stress) then:

* Use YINERGY™ Eugesterone 1/4 tsp. on the skin twice a day.
* Take YINERGY Essentials 4/day.
* Take YINERGY Youth Formula 4/day.
* Use YINERGY Oil. As for healthy people use for six weeks and recheck DHEA.

Then if your DHEA is below 600 as a man or below 450 as a woman, have your physician write a prescription for a Liss TENS (available from Self Health Systems 417-267-2900, FAX 417-267-3102) for use on the Ring of Fire. Use it daily for 3 months and then recheck DHEA.

For men with DHEA below 180 ng/dL or women below 130 ng/dL, do all five approaches for 3 months while taking 100 mg/day of DHEA (for men) and 50 mg/day (for women). After 3 months, cut DHEA in half for 2 weeks, cut in another half for 2 weeks, and then stop DHEA. Continue all five restoration approaches. Six weeks later recheck DHEA to be certain you are now well above 180 (men) or 130 (women).

EXCEPTIONS:

Women with breast, uterine, or ovarian cancer or men with prostate cancer should NOT take DHEA. They may use all five restoration techniques.

Other than those truly deficient (men below 180 and women below 130)

UNDER NO CIRCUMSTANCES

should you take DHEA.

Other natural, health enhancing ways to optimize DHEA:

*   BE HAPPY AND LAUGH 5 minutes 3 times
    daily. (Laughing Meditation Tape available from
    Self Health Systems 417-267-2900, FAX 417-267-
    3102)
*   EXERCISE - Build to 10 minutes of limbering
    exercises (see 90 DAYS TO STRESS-FREE
    LIVING available from Self-Health Systems, 417-
    267-2900, FAX 417-267-3102) and 45 to 50
    minutes of brisk walking.
*   ENJOY SEX - Even fun, sexual fantasies are
    good.
*   BE OUTSIDE 1 hour per day.
*   If you work inside all days and/or are exposed to
    a lot of electronic equipment - computers,
    printers, cars, planes, etc. - get and wear a Q
    Pendant (available from Self Health Systems 417-
    267-2900, FAX 417-267-3109).

CHAPTER 6

MAGNESIUM: THE ESSENTIAL MINERAL
CRITICAL FOR YOUTH AND HEALTH

Magnesium is the most critical mineral required for electrical stability of every cell in the body. Its major role is at and in the cells so that blood levels, whole blood, serum, plasma, and even white blood cell levels of magnesium do not give an accurate picture of optimal magnesium levels. In fact, serum levels of magnesium are low only in acute alcoholics and in severe starvation. Magnesium stored in bones is "stolen" by the body to maintain the narrow range of serum levels required for life.

Eighty percent of American women and seventy percent of men do not eat even the recommended daily requirement of magnesium. And soil throughout the world is deficient in magnesium except in Egypt. Thus, most foods today, even those supposed to have a high content of magnesium, are low themselves. As a single essential nutrient, magnesium may be responsible for more diseases than any other nutrient! There are many reasons for this widespread deficiency: nutrition, stress and drugs. White flour has had removed 85% of its magnesium. Considering the fact that almost 20% of calories come from white flour, essentially a junk food, this inadequate food is responsible for about 17% "loss" of magnesium. Chemical fertilizers, high in nitrates, phosphates, and potassium, deplete soil magnesium so that even most whole wheat is basically borderline.

Farmers are well aware of the major impact of magnesium depletion; horses and cattle may die from "grass staggers," an uncoordinated gait, severe muscle spasms and even seizures. All this is curable by magnesium supplementation, if caught early enough.

The second junk food which has no magnesium, and indeed no real nutritional value, is white sugar. The average American consumes 42 teaspoons of sugar per day, 210 calories, or about 10% of caloric intake.

Add 15%, minimum, for protein and 35% for fat, both lacking in magnesium, and it is obvious that at least 77% of our food has no magnesium. Furthermore, both fat and protein interfere with absorption of magnesium.

And then there is that enigma of modern life, "pop," which is phosphate of soda, a major stumbling block in magnesium metabolism. At an average of 24 to 36 oz. per day, the ultimate junk non-food, pop, is one of the unsung, unrecognized villains in disease promotion.

Other major magnesium detractors include the 550,000 different chemical pollutants released every year into our air, soil and water. Pesticides, herbicides, and ammonia, widely used in agriculture, seriously stress the body, affecting every aspect of metabolism. One of the major pollutants is aluminum which blocks many normal magnesium functions. Aluminum, the non-essential and highly toxic mineral, is used to wrap foods and to store pop, beer and even juice. The acid pH of many juices and of pop leaches aluminum out of the containers. And to compound matters, antiperspirants and most baking powder contains aluminum. Any of the toxic metals, aluminum, cadmium, lead, arsenic, and mercury may block magnesium metabolism.

In addition, the clinical stressors mentioned above

contribute to the overall stress reaction - an increase in "adrenalin," cortisone, blood sugar, and insulin. And both adrenalin and cortisone lead to increased excretion of magnesium in the urine. Noise and electromagnetic pollution also elicit this biochemical stress reaction leading to magnesium dumping. And then there is the Future Shock of modern life. All emotional/mental stress further aggravates the adrenalin, cortisone induced magnesium depletion.

And to compound the remarkable attack upon magnesium, there is a huge arsenal of prescription drugs that deplete magnesium. These include most diuretics, hydrochlorothiazide, chlorthalidone, furosemide, bumetanide; antibiotics - gentamicin, carbenicillin, amphotericin B; cortisone/steroid drugs such as prednisone and dexamethasone; digitalis/digoxin; antiasthmatics including ephedrine and pseudophedrine; laxatives; chemo therapeutics - cisplatin, vinblastine, bleomycin, cyclosporine, methotrexate, etc. And, of course, those non-prescriptions - nicotine and alcohol. It's a near miracle that we survive in modern society!

Stress begets stress. The lower your magnesium

level, the lower your threshold for new stress - thus, you become increasingly more sensitive - more adrenalin, greater magnesium loss, greater sensitivity, etc. Soon the intracellular magnesium level is no longer 10 times that of serum and the cells are in a chronic state of hyperexcitability. Anxiety, irritability, anger, depression and mood swings are just the tip of the iceberg of magnesium deficient symptoms:

Anxiety

Attention Deficit

Confusion

Depression

Diarrhea or Constipation

Faintness

Fatigue

Hyperventilation

Incoordination

Insomnia

Intestinal Problems

Muscle Cramps

Muscle Tightness

Muscle Twitches

Pain

Poor Memory

Seizures

Tinnitus

Vertigo

THESE ARE JUST THE SYMPTOMS! Major diseases associated with magnesium deficiency are:

Angina Pectoris

Anorexia

Arrhythmias

Asthma

Atherosclerosis

Attention Deficit Disorder

Auricular Fibrillation

Bulimia

Cancer

Cardiomyopathy

Chronic Fatigue

Chronic Bronchitis

Congestive Heart Failure

Cirrhosis

Depression

Diabetes

Eclampsia

Emphysema

Fibromyalgia

Gall Bladder Infections and Stones

Hearing Loss

Heart Attack

Hyperactivity

Hypercholesterolemia

Hypertension

Hypoglycemia

Immune Deficiency

Infections (Viral and Bacterial)

Intermittent Claudication

Kidney Stones

Migraine

Mitral Valve Prolapse

Osteoporosis

Panic Attacks

PMS - Pre menstrual syndrome

Benign Prostatic Hypertrophy

PVC's

Reflex Sympathetic Dystrophy

Strokes

In perhaps no illness is magnesium deficiency more relevant than myocardial infarction or acute heart attack. On average, patients given intravenous magnesium have a 50% greater survival rate than those who do not receive magnesium. No drug is more effective than magnesium in reducing mortality from a heart attack. No drug is as safe. Indeed, I consider failure to give magnesium to such a patient significant negligence.

Another major disease in which magnesium deficiency is rampant is diabetes. Just glucosuria, the spilling of sugar in urine, depletes magnesium. Indeed there is an inverse relationship between glycosuria and serum magnesium. In severe diabetic crisis with ketoacidosis, extreme magnesium loss is common.

More critically, magnesium is an important co-factor in production of insulin by the pancreas. Normal TOTAL BODY magnesium is essential for glucose metabolism. Thus, the rampant magnesium deficiency in our society may be a contributing CAUSE of diabetes.

121

Insulin resistance, muscle spasms, atherosclerosis, cardiac arrhythmias, and even the increase in vascular disease in diabetes may be related to magnesium deficiency.

Another heart-rending illness, cerebral palsy, may be the result of magnesium deficiency. Mothers given intravenous magnesium just before giving birth are much less likely to have children who develop cerebral palsy.

MIGRAINE

Migraine, a disabling condition for 12 to 13% of Americans (17% of women; 9% of men), is associated with magnesium deficiency in most patients. As effective as most drugs is a shot of magnesium given at the onset of the headache. And long-term magnesium supplementation reduces the frequency of migraines.

HYPERTENSION

Both calcium deficiency (70% of patients) and magnesium deficiency (80%) are important factors in hypertension. Indeed, adequate replacement of both calcium and magnesium may make antihypertensive drugs unnecessary.

CHRONIC FATIGUE SYNDROME AND FIBROMYALGIA

Chronic fatigue syndrome and fibromyalgia are two modern illnesses frustrating both patients and most physicians. Neither is likely to be cured without AT LEAST adequate magnesium replacement.

DEPRESSION

In hundreds of depressed patients, magnesium deficiency is almost universal. Magnesium replacement is one of the key elements for long-term success in this perhaps most common illness in the world. Indeed, I believe depression is a key factor which weakens resistance to all illness and is at least a major co-factor in almost every illness.

OSTEOPOROSIS

One of the most difficult oversights by physicians is the role of magnesium in bone maintenance and production. Just as magnesium increases the strength of concrete, magnesium is absolutely critical to formation of both bone and teeth. It is the unique chemical combination of calcium and magnesium that makes bones and teeth sound. Interestingly, a small amount of boron is also essential in bone metabolism, as of course is Vitamin D. No amount of estrogen and calcium is adequate for prevention or treatment of osteoporosis without magnesium, boron and Vitamin D. Of course, my personal recommendation is daily 1/2 teaspoon of YINERGY™ EUGESTERONE™ (transdermally), 400 units of Vitamin D, one gram of calcium citrate, and adequate magnesium, either as magnesium taurate or YINERGY™ oil.

PANIC ATTACKS AND RSD

Both panic attacks and reflex sympathetic dystrophy are disabling diseases which are often curable with just 10 to 15 shots of magnesium intravenously. Indeed, except for patients with kidney failure, there is virtually no illness which is not helped significantly by magnesium.

Now to address the two biggest problems with magnesium deficiency: diagnosis and replacement.

DIAGNOSIS OF MAGNESIUM DEFICIENCY

Serum or blood levels of magnesium are a waste of blood, money and time except in acute alcoholism, starvation or diabetic acidosis. There are only two tests worthwhile: magnesium loading and intracellular spectroscopy.

MAGNESIUM LOADING

Although this test is considered the standard by the few physicians who at least recognize the possibility of magnesium deficiency, the test is somewhat tedious and frustrating to patients. First one has to collect every drop of urine for exactly 24 hours. The urine is then analyzed for total magnesium and creatinine output. Then the patient is given intravenously a specific "load" of magnesium and a second 24 hour urine is collected and tested for magnesium and creatinine. If less than 50% of the administered magnesium is excreted, this is "proof" of magnesium deficiency. In fact, if less than 20% is excreted, "borderline" magnesium deficiency is suspected.

INTRACELLULAR SPECTROSCOPY

Much simpler and the test I prefer is a simple tongue blade scraping of the frenulum of the tongue. Then the cells are placed on a slide and sent for x-ray defraction. At about the same cost as the magnesium load test and much better patient compliance, this test also gives intracellular levels of magnesium, calcium, potassium, sodium, chloride, and phosphorus, as well as equally important ratios. If your physician won't order this important test for you, find another physician. If you have any of the symptoms or illnesses listed earlier, it is extremely wise to have this test done. The lab is: Intracellular Diagnostics, 553 Pilgrim Drive, Suite B, Commerce Park, Foster City, CA 94404, 800-874-4804.

MAGNESIUM REPLACEMENT

Except in patients with kidney failure, some magnesium supplementation is advisable. The problem with oral magnesium is that all magnesium compounds are potentially laxative. And there is good evidence that magnesium absorption depends upon the mineral remaining in the intestine at least 12 hours. If intestinal transit time is less than 12 hours, magnesium absorption is impaired. There are two oral forms that may be considered: 25% magnesium chloride drops (Magic Drops) or magnesium taurate. The drops are extremely strong tasting, salty and bitter. At least 50% of patients refuse to use the drops after a taste test! Twenty drops per day are recommended. It requires 3 to 6 months for replacement to be accomplished.

Magnesium taurate at dosages of 250 to 500 mg., if well tolerated (no diarrhea) by the intestines, is better absorbed than any other oral tablet or capsule. This approach requires 6 to 12 months.

INTRAVENOUS MAGNESIUM

The most rapid restoration of intracellular magnesium is accomplished with intravenous replacement. For most patients 10 shots, given over a two week period, are adequate. Depending upon the patient's weight and general status, we give either 1 or 2 grams of magnesium chloride IV over a 30 to 60 minute period.

MAGNESIUM I

250 cc of 0.9% Sodium Chloride

1 gram Magnesium Chloride

500 mg Calcium Chloride

100 mg. Pyridoxine (B-6)

1 gram DexPanthenol (B-5)

1000 mcg Cyanocobalamin (B-12

6 grams Vitamin C

MAGNESIUM II

250 cc of 0.9% Sodium Chloride

2 grams Magnesium Chloride

1 gram Calcium Chloride

100 mg. Pyridoxine (B-6)

1 gram DexPanthenol (B-5)

1000 mcg Cyanocobalamin (B-12

6 grams Vitamin C

In patients with panic attacks, as few as 5 intravenous replacements may be sufficient. In reflex sympathetic dystrophy, as many as 15 shots may be required. Once replacement is completed, most individuals may be able to sustain their magnesium levels with oral magnesium taurate. But a few patients require occasional additional intravenous magnesium replacements.

MAGIC OIL, YINERGY OIL™, ESSENCE OF SEA OIL, CELL WELLNESS RESTORER™

In considering the wide variety of illnesses reported by Jim Carter to be improved with his unusual oil, I suspected that one explanation might be magnesium replacement. This insight led me to test the possibility that the oil, known to contain up to 25% magnesium chloride might facilitate absorption of magnesium through the skin. We then recruited 16 individuals with low intracellular magnesium levels to participate in the following experiment. The protocol/consent form explaining study this study is as follows:

Our purpose was to research whether or not magnesium was absorbed through the skin. Exclusion factors included anyone taking oral or IV magnesium during the last 6 weeks and smokers. Individuals sprayed a solution of 50% Magic Oil over the entire body once daily for a month and did a 20 minute foot soak in Magic Oil once daily for a month. Subjects had a baseline Intracellular Magnesium Test documenting their deficiency and another post-Intracellular Magnesium Test after 1 month of daily soaks.

The results were impressive. Twelve of sixteen patients, 75%, had significant improvements in intracellular magnesium levels after only four weeks of foot soaking and skin spraying.

TYPICAL RESULTS

Before Foot Soaking (mEq/l)		Reference Range (mEq/l)
Magnesium	31.4	33.9 - 41.9
Calcium	7.5	3.2 - 5.0
Potassium	132.2	80.0 - 240.0
Sodium	3.4	3.8 - 5.8
Chloride	3.2	3.4 - 6.0
Phosphorus	22.2	14.2 - 17.0
Phosphorus/Cal.	3.0	3.5 - 4.3
Magnesium/Cal.	4.2	7.8 - 10.9
Magnesium/Phosp.	1.4	1.8 - 3.0
Potassium/Cal.	17.6	25.8 - 52.4
Potassium/Magnes.	4.2	2.4 - 4.6
Potassium/Sod.	39.1	21.5 - 44.6

After 4 Weeks Foot Soaking (mEq/l)		Reference Range (mEq/l)
Magnesium	41.2	33.9 - 41.9
Calcium	4.8	3.2 - 5.0
Potassium	124.5	80.0 - 240.0
Sodium	4.1	3.8 - 5.8
Chloride	3.4	3.4 - 6.0
Phosphorus	17.6	14.2 - 17.0
Phosphorus/Cal.	3.7	3.5 - 4.3
Magnesium/Cal.	8.6	7.8 - 10.9
Magnesium/Phosp.	2.3	1.8 - 3.0
Potassium/Cal.	26.1	25.8 - 52.4
Potassium/Magnes.	3.0	2.4 - 4.6
Potassium/Sod.	30.5	21.5 - 44.6

This is the first known proof of absorption of magnesium through the skin! And it suggests that 70% of individuals Jim Carter reports improved with use of his unique oil improved because of increased intracellular magnesium. FROM A SAFETY POINT OF VIEW, THERE IS NO OTHER APPROACH THAT OFFERS SO MUCH TO SO MANY. Not only is this great news for individuals with all the symptoms and illnesses listed earlier, it is also a reason in itself to recommend use of Cell Wellness Restorer™ or YINERGY Oil™ in everyone with normal kidney function. Considering the many reports of improved health, energy and well being, Magic Oil may BE the Fountain of Youth.

CHAPTER 7

CLINICAL EXPERIENCES

On my first visit to Jim Carter and the Star Chamber in the Fall of 1998, I met Rochelle. She was born May 22, 1948 and at age 50, looked considerably younger than her stated age. When she showed me photographs of herself taken nine months earlier, it was difficult to believe that it was the same person. Her story is perhaps one of the most striking I have encountered in the 48 years since I entered medical school. Rochelle, President and Founder of Star Babies Preferred, LLC, considered herself to be healthy and free of significant problems until December 20, 1996. She had walked into a bank as a customer. The teller looked up and asked her to come forward. She was the only customer in the bank at the time. The teller looked down and up and said "that's funny." He was still working on previous paperwork. As Rochelle was trying to figure out what the teller was laughing about, a man grabbed her by the hair, pulling her to the right and backwards and held an approximately 12 inch kitchen knife tightly against her left neck. He kept asking the teller to give him $20's and $50's. Eventually about the fourth time Rochelle screamed "give him the money." She heard a lot of voices about that time and the teller was giving the robber packets of $20 bills while the robber kept jerking her further to the right and back. When he got a packet of $50's, the robber suddenly threw her to the right and back and left the bank. Rochelle says that she was treated as if she were a criminal or an accomplice of the robber by the people at the bank.

This was a critical day in Rochelle's life. It was the day in which her husband who had been treated with chemotherapy for lung cancer was in remission and they were to celebrate that. Rochelle's health deteriorated so instantly and completely that she feels that was a significant factor in her husband's relapse and death on December 27, 1997. She felt it was the last straw for her husband. She had always been the great caretaker spending great amounts of time with him, etc. Now from the moment of that abuse by the robber, she developed a wide variety of problems. She went into menopausal symptoms, felt as if a fire was raging in her, and she felt as if she would explode from the heat. She began to have panic attacks as if she would shake apart. She developed pains from head to toe and migraines so severe that she felt her head would explode. She developed diarrhea and vomiting that lasted over the next 14 months. She would have diarrhea 8 to 12 times a day and vomiting at least every morning. Her head felt heavy, especially around the right neck and head and shoulders. She walked hunched over, had multiple spasms throughout her body and charley horses. Even if she took a deep breath she would go into spasms. She ground her teeth together because of pain. Her teeth got out of line and she kept biting her tongue and cheek but because her husband was getting more and more ill, she did not visit a dentist. She was totally de-energized, at times not able to get out of bed. Having weighed about 150 lbs. prior to the event at the bank, she rapidly gained 40 lbs. and then stopped weighing herself. She doesn't know exactly where she wound up. She felt paranoid. Many people said she was hysterical and out of control. There was no position in which she could lie comfortably. She had great insomnia and tremendous nightmares. She began to lose hair. She was puffy and had black bags under her eyes. She says she looked as if she was 12 months pregnant. She had no ability to concentrate. Her toenails began to split and her fingernails became thick and ugly. Her feet were cracked and hard. She had black and brown spots all over her skin and her skin was sagging and leathery. She looked 70 to 80 years old. She lost her job working as a chiropractic assistant. Interestingly, she had had no medical care other than chiropractic for the previous 25 years.

During the summer of 1997 while she was at her worst but trying to hold on as her husband became increasingly ill, Rochelle met Jim Carter through an acquaintance. She began using some of his Magic Water and would rub the Magic Oil on her skin, sometimes rubbing it in for up to two hours with some slight relief of pain but her life continued to crash around her up through the time of her husband's death in December 1997.

Then in February 1998, Jim invited her to try his

new creation, the Star Chamber. He allowed her in the tub for 10 minutes. She felt giddy and euphoric and full of energy. She had been crying almost steadily for almost 13 months and that stopped. A positive attitude appeared instantly. Her skin became instantly softer. The wrinkles began to be less obvious. Diarrhea decreased. She had had a migraine for two days at that time and it was gone when she came out of the Star Chamber. Her right neck and shoulder pain diminished and the charley horses were decreased. She slept better, in fact some seven hours that night with less nightmares. She lost three pounds of weight and felt less puffy.

The following day she spent 30 minutes in the Star Chamber. She came out feeling bubbly with a marked increase in energy and less paranoia. A lump under her right arm had diminished in size. She slept much better and felt and looked younger. She gained one pound that day but her appetite was better and she was drinking less water. Her diarrhea and stomach pain markedly diminished. The charley horses interestingly moved into her left side where they had been less dominant than on the right before this. On the third day,

she was allowed on the Black Crystal Bed for 20
minutes, in the tub for 20 minutes, and on the Laminar
Crystal Bed for 20 minutes. That was March 4, 1998.
She felt euphoric, more serene and hungry when she
came out. The charley horse, however, around her left
knee increased but the wrinkles and the bags under the
eyes were further decreasing. She lost a pound. She had
diarrhea ten times that day but felt better mentally and
concentrated better. She had frequent visits to the Star
Chamber over the next week and on March 12th at 8:00
a.m. she threw up mucus the size of a softball. She
could hardly take herself away from the sink but her eyes
were less puffy, the wrinkles were decreasing, the brown
spots were fading, her hair felt soft and thicker and on
March 14, 1998, she had her tenth visit to the Star
Chamber. For the first time since the assault in the
bank, she had a normal bowel movement. On the 15th
of March 1998, she met two Catholic brothers who knew
her well some six plus months earlier but who did not
recognize her when she came up to them in Lake Tahoe.

Within two weeks of her beginning in the Star
Chamber, Rochelle began to notice that many people

were not recognizing her. Within three months of initiating the Star Chamber experience, she began buying new clothes and over about a six month period, she lost some 65 lbs., going down to a size six, "a size I never was able to get into in my life before." Rochelle continued occasional but not nearly so frequent visits to the Star Chamber but her life otherwise has changed markedly.

LIVING THE CRYSTAL LIFE

She sleeps on 1,000 pounds of the laminar crystal or carries with her a sleeping bag filled with crystals on which she sleeps when she travels. In her Jacuzzi^R she has 300 gallons of Magic Water using 50 of the ceramic "cupcakes" as well as some Prills in her Jacuzzi. She has a Prill shower converter so that when she takes a shower she gets Magic Water. She uses Prill water for douches or colonics, the latter about twice a month. She drinks only crystal water made with the ceramic cupcake. She likes that somewhat better as it is sweeter than the Prill water. She uses a bag of prills in her washing machine and has not used detergent or water softener for two years. She cooks with Crystal Water. She treats all of her food with Crystal Water leaving it on a box of the crystals until it ripens. Oranges will keep up to a couple of months on the crystals and taste much sweeter than those that have not been on it. All of her food is treated with the crystals: spices, cereals, soups, everything. When she uses canned goods, she dilutes them with crystal water. When she uses frozen juices they are reconstituted with Crystal Water. She has even put the Magic Oil in her ears and it has helped to gradually get rid of the feeling of one of her ears being swollen shut.

She is not back totally to what she was prior to the assault in the bank. She still has some up and down days. She still has a little bit of throat mucous but in other ways she is much better than she was. Her hair, which had turned rapidly gray, has gone back to almost totally normal red. She feels as if she would unquestionably not be alive if it had not been for meeting Jim and her experiences with the Star Chamber and the water/oil products that Jim has made.

Looking back to the day when she was first invited to try the Star Chamber, Jim told her about it and about the black crystal bed on which she would lie before going into the tub. She asked, "What is the downside?" The answer was, "you just might blow up." She said, "I am going for it. I have nothing to lose." And, indeed, she has regained, youth, health and enthusiasm.

A PERSONAL STAR CHAMBER EXPERIENCE

My personal experience in the Star Chamber occurred some three to four hours after I had first met Jim. We had sat in his office talking while he gave me a bit of the history. I sprayed my face several times with Magic Water and felt somewhat rejuvenated. I then lay down on the black gold iodide crystal bed. It was certainly as hard as concrete. I had some trouble relaxing on it but eventually did. I think I lay there for some 20 minutes. I then was allowed to go into the Star Tub where I believe they placed 8 oz. of Magic Oil. It was very interesting. Usually when I get into a tub of hot water, I want to relax and fall asleep but I could hardly stay still. I kept moving about, splashing the water and being very energetic with both my arms and legs. After the allotted time in the tub, I was allowed out to lie on the Laminar Crystal Bed. Again, it took me a little while to relax but I fell into a deep state of relaxation.

It was now well past my usual dinner time and yet I had not been hungry throughout the afternoon. Jim and I went out to eat and I ate relatively little. I slept on the Laminar Crystal Bed that night and it was very hard. I had some of the most vivid dreams I have ever had in my life. I awoke the next morning, however, feeling reasonably refreshed and had another trip through the Black Crystal Bed, the pool, and the Laminar Crystal Bed and felt totally rejuvenated and energized. I was not hungry. Finally at about noon that day as I got back to the airport, I had a small meal. I went from Boulder City to St. Louis where I immediately attended a conference and as in most hotels, there was no tub in which to take a soak so I instead sprayed myself with the Magic Water and rubbed on some of the oil and then took a shower every day.

My appetite seemed down for a week. I lost 2 lbs. without trying. I took baths almost daily over a period of three to six months using 2 and up to 16 ounces of the oil. I always felt extremely relaxed and re-energized. Having been very healthy otherwise, it is hard for me to make any other personal statements except that it is quite common for people who have not seen me in a year or so to talk about how young I look. As I see myself in the mirror everyday, it is much harder for me to tell!

OBSERVATIONS BY DR. ROBERT GOODMAN PRESIDENT OF NUCCA:

Dear Dr. Shealy: I appreciate this opportunity to express my observations of Jim Carter's amazing natural remedies. I applaud the natural health care philosophy you have developed which is light years away from your original educational process. It would be hard to get from there to here. You have done well to positively affect the lives of so many people around the world. I wish you and Jim the best in your endeavor. I also hope that someday you could experience the precision spinal aligning technique I call NUCCA. I truly believe that we have another piece of the puzzle.

Introduction: Dr. Robert Goodman is the owner and CEO of the Nevada Spine Center in the Las Vegas area. The Nevada Spine Center is a natural health care facility. Dr. Goodman has seen patients from 42 states and 15 foreign countries. He has been published in research journals for his work with hypertension, epileptic seizures, Attention Deficit Disorder, and delayed childhood development. He is the President of an international group of Chiropractic physicians called NUCCA (National Upper Cervical Chiropractic Association). Dr. Goodman has tried or tested over 300 health care and nutritional products. He has been to 30 countries and has presented seminars around the U.S. and Canada.

Text: Have you ever asked yourself these questions, "Why are children so flexible and have so much energy? And why are adults so still and tired?" Most of our diseases today are degenerative, like the many forms of arthritis, impaired bowel functions, blocked lymphatic drainage, or arteriosclerosis. These conditions are all due to a lack of fluid communication. When the juices stop flowing, life stops happening.

In a book called BODYWISE written in 1986, the author states, "All living things are characterized by their fluid flow; they express their health by the greatest possible fluidity. The process of life may be seen as a

144

process of drying up, drying out, or being hung up to dry. In the course of aging, most of us find ourselves sedentary, moving less and less. We may claim this static state results from pain, fatigue, or laziness, but which comes first, the pain and fatigue or the lack of fluid communication?"

The lack of fluid communication decreases your body's ability to absorb and utilize vitamins, minerals, and nutrients. The lack of fluid communication decreases our ability to eliminate waste products causing toxic build up that further decreases fluid flow and slows down the chemical processes we use to create energy.

What if we had a process or product that could reverse the "drying up" condition we call aging? What if we had something that could re-hydrate the body and restore proper absorption, elimination, and energy building processes? Can you actually imagine a real true-to-life anti-aging technique and what that would mean to the world?

For 24 years I have searched for a product, method, or technique that would do just that. Five years ago I began to experiment with Jim Carter's unique substances. Jim is an awake person; one who exhibits that common thread of knowledge and technology shared by some of the great contributors the world has known throughout history. I have tested his hypotheses of human restoration on myself, my family, and my patients. These two products, Crystal Water and Crystal Oil, have proven to be the most amazing natural remedies I have ever tried or tested. In my opinion, these products are a combination of advanced scientific technology and re-discovered ancient wisdom. The following is a sample of my own clinical results and patient testimonials.

Overall, patients have reported to me the following symptomatic changes after using the Crystal Oil and Crystal Water:

Immediate pain relief

Relief of chronic arthritic pain throughout the body

Increased flexibility

Improved immune function (relief of allergies, less infections, decreased episodes of colds and flu)

146

Lower cholesterol

Lower blood pressure

Better sleep

Increased energy and clarity

Relief of menstrual cramps

More youthful appearance

Repair of damaged and aged skin

Less wrinkles

Relief of knee and other joint pain

Relief of rashes and other skin problems

Sun protection and relief from sun burn and other burns

Relief from pulled muscles

Gets rid of cellulite and detoxes other waste products

Some people lose weight

Relief of sprain/strain injuries

In December 1999, a 49 year old female entered my office suffering from severe neck pain and muscular spasms due to a recent whiplash injury. After examination and x-ray, I sprayed her neck with the Crystal Water and the pain resolved within one minute.

Between appointments, the patient used the Crystal Water each time she felt pain or stiffness. The irritation resolved each time for several hours.

In December 1999, a 31 year old female presented to my office suffering from joint pain throughout most of her body. She had been diagnosed with Fibromyalgia. Beginning in the fall of each year, she would contract colds and the flu which would continue through most of the winter. Along with Chiropractic care, she was instructed to use the Crystal Oil and Crystal Water. By April 2000, she had not had a cold or flu for 3 months and the chronic joint pain had improved by 90%.

In January 2000, a 35 year old female presented to my office with a rash on her head, neck and chest. She had been to a dermatologist three times in the last six months, was given more than one prescription, and still had no relief. She began spraying the affected areas with the Crystal Water and within 24 hours the rash was gone.

A professional bowler presented unable to fully flex the ring finger of his right hand. He had injured it 10 years ago and had not been able to fully bend it since that time. After spraying his finger several times in one afternoon, he was able to fully flex and straighten his finger.

A 45 year old female patient was given the Crystal Oil to use in a bath. After six baths, she had lost 8 pounds and her cellulite was completely gone.

A 22 year old female presented to my office with a diagnosis of interstitial cystitis which is an irritation of the abdominal tract, especially the bladder. It can be very painful and the symptoms are exacerbated by stimulants and spicy foods. The symptoms persisted after Chiropractic care, so the patient was instructed to use the Crystal Oil and Crystal Water. Her pain and symptoms have been resolved for six months and her dietary restrictions have decreased as well.

My father is 76 years old. He has a lumbar scoliosis which has affected his walk and created left knee pain and clicking of the joint. The pain persisted after Chiropractic care. An orthopedic examination and possible surgery could have been our next step. Instead, I instructed him to use the Crystal Oil every day. He would rub a tablespoon on the affected area each time.

The knee pain and clicking resolved within a few weeks and he is now able to ride a stationary bike and walk up stairs without any problems.

N. J. - "The Crystal Water helps almost instantly with pain. My muscles relax and my pain is better. Soaking in the Crystal Oil is very relaxing and calming. I'm a fibromyalgia sufferer and usually spend my winters miserable with the cold and flu, but no longer! For the first time in years I had only one mild cold."

K. R. - "My body was in such a weakened state, the Immune 700 has helped me up and my daily illness has not returned once since taking it. I've also been using the Crystal Water, as well as the Crystal Oil to relieve the chronic pain in my knees. Taking walks has become fun again!"

S. C. - "After having lost 10 pounds, the Crystal Oil has helped my skin feel soft and toned. It also detoxed by body, I feel radiant!"

D. A. - "My skin has gotten wrinkled over the years and I had terrible problems with bruising. By soaking in the Crystal Oil, my whole body has smoothed out, become younger, and I no longer get the ugly bruises."

M. B. - "Dear Dr. Goodman, the Crystal Oil has helped my arthritis and I swear by it. However, something happened last weekend that convinced me it's not a placebo effect. I was leading our six-year-old granddaughter, Alex, on our horse when something spooked it and it tried to jerk away from me. Alex was thrown down hard on the rocky ground. There were abrasions and welts on her side and hip, and she could no longer put any weight on her left leg. I was so afraid she was permanently injured. I carried her to the house and immediately put her in a warm bath with 4 oz. of the Crystal Oil. It was evident that Alex was going to be just a mass of bruises in the morning. After 20 minutes, Alex stepped out of the bath herself, was able to walk normally, and never had one bruise on her body! I don't know how it works, and I don't care because one thing is for sure, the Crystal Oil is definitely miraculous."

N. W. - "I was skeptical about my first results with the Crystal Oil and Crystal Water, even though they were the only products to give me relief from my allergies and severe fatigue. However, soon I noticed relief from my eye strain as well as a greatly improved complexion. My husband was upset because now I look younger than he does! I decided to try the Crystal Oil in a little different way. For years I have suffered with violent headaches that seem to be sinus related. They make me completely non-functional and require heavy medication to get any sleep. I feel the characteristic pain behind my eyes, across my face and temples, and down my neck. During my last bout, I poured a little of the Crystal Oil on my finger and put it around my sinus area, temples, neck and shoulders. It stung a bit at first, but the headache pain eased some, within a few minutes there was only a slight ache, and after 10 minutes the pain was completely gone! I didn't get another attack for several weeks, I applied the Crystal Oil again and lo and behold it worked again!"

P. W. - "I was pleasantly amazed when a little of the Crystal Water that I rubbed on my stomach actually helped ease my painful menstrual cramps!"

D. B. - "When I was 15, the doctors told me I had interstitial cystitis, and that I would have to learn to live with it. My bladder burned so bad all the time that I was irritable and in enough pain some days to cry. Cutting out the acidic foods helped but I was still in real pain. Dr. Goodman suggested I begin using the Crystal Oil, so I started soaking every night for a couple of weeks. I also began to use the Immune 700. Well, it's been six months and I feel great. I believe the Crystal Oil, Crystal Water and Immune 700 are effective in relieving pain and gave me back the energy and clarity in my life. There are a lot of women who have suffered longer than 7 years, but if I could tell them one thing it would be to try these products, you have nothing to lose but the suffering."

D. B. - "I knew my body had collected so much toxicity over the years, I think we all do. The Crystal Oil has cleared that right out of me. I feel I have a fresh new body to take to work everyday."

C. H. - "The Crystal Oil is wonderful. I am finally able to move without stiffness immediately after soaking and at last I can relax without pain. The Crystal Water has also helped with the fibromyalgia pain I've had for years. It also removed pain from sunburn and other injuries."

K. T. - "This is about the first time I ever used - Crystal Oil, now I use it for just about everything!!

I had quit smoking for a week or so when a bump came up on the top of my foot (I don't know if that had anything to do with the bump or not). It just kept getting bigger and bigger and it was so sore that I could not wear any of my shoes. The pain it was causing was very bad and it started swelling and getting really red and looked very infected all the way up to my ankle. Well, to make a long, painful story short, I went to 5 different doctors, who all called it something different; one lanced it and then they ended up calling it a wound infection! I never found out what it was and after 3 rounds of antibiotics and 5 doctors and 6 weeks later and not being able to go to work from the swelling and pain, I called Dr. Goodman. He said "I have something I want you to try." So he sent me the Crystal Oil (I live in Oklahoma) and told me to soak my foot in it 3 times a day. I thought, yeah right, that is really going to help it, but I did exactly what he told me to do and 3 days later it was totally and completely healed! I wish I had taken pictures because my family and I could not believe it. I kept expecting it to come back but not only did it not come back, I had athlete's foot in between two toes on that foot that flared up about once or twice a month and it has been nine months and not a sign of it!

I have many of experiences I could tell about how this has healed different ailments in my family but I would have to write a 10-page letter. I just want to say I have never seen anything like the Crystal Oil, and the Crystal Water has stories of its own. I want to thank you for introducing me to both."

These are reports by a licensed Doctor of Chiropractic. Obviously they are the result of professional experience. In addition, we have seen scores of reports from individuals. A few of these follow.

ADDITIONAL REPORTS FROM INDIVIDUALS WHO HAVE USED MAGIC OIL AND/OR WATER

S. H. - "On Thursday April 6, 2000, I stepped off a 3' shelf and landed wrong, wrenching my ankle. In the process, I managed to tear all the ligaments and tendons on both sides of the right ankle making it extremely difficult to put pressure on it, and walk for that matter. On that Friday I went to the doctor. At first assessment, he thought it was fractured. After the x-rays revealed that there was no break, he proceeded to tape it up and immobilize it. The following day D. M. returned from Las Vegas with a wonderful oil called Cell Wellness Restorer. Early that morning, Saturday, April 8, 2000, D. M. rubbed the oil on my ankle. Within 20 minutes I was up and about walking around with little or no pain. I was amazed to say the least, as was Doug. I have since been using the oil on a regular basis. On another note, the doctor said 6 weeks, 2 weeks with crutches. After only 1 week using Cell Wellness Restorer, I'm virtually 100% no pain, no crutches, no problem."

M. H. - "I first became aware of Jim Carter's crystal approximately 7 years ago. Jim gave me a few ceramic pieces containing the crystal and told me to experiment with water and to 'have fun.'

My sister had been suffering from gastrointestinal problems for many years and was unable to eat any raw fruits or vegetables. I gave her one of the ceramic stones. She placed the stone in a pitcher and would then drink the water. She soon was able to eat raw fruits and vegetables. She continues to drink the water every day.

I was preparing to travel to Nevada to meet with Jim. I had a cold that then turned to pneumonia. This was a familiar pattern for me. In my youth, I suffered from asthma. Since the age of 18, every time I would get a cold, it would soon drop to my chest and I would get pneumonia. This would happen once or twice each year. I went to the doctor for some antibiotics. He said my lungs were very congested and that if I didn't get some rest, he would put me in the hospital. He gave me a shot of penicillin and told me to call him if I had any problems. I called Jim and told him of my sickness and that I would have to delay my trip. He told me to take the ceramic plate he'd given me and place it on my chest, alternating sides of my chest for about 20 minutes per side. I did this throughout the evening. I noticed that my lungs would become very cold, but the plate and my chest remained at room temperature. Since the cold temperature was very soothing, I continued to keep the plate on my chest. The next morning I awoke feeling great. I returned to the doctor with my daughter; he had to listen to my lungs and make sure I didn't need to be hospitalized. I kept insisting that I felt great. He was baffled when my lungs appeared to be totally clear. He offered to take x-rays at his expense. He then showed me the new x-rays compared to those he had taken the day before. The difference was dramatic. One set showed lungs full of "stuff" - the other showed lungs totally clear. He said he'd never seen anyone respond so quickly to penicillin.

In the past 7 years, I have had 2 colds and no pneumonia. Both colds came at times when I was traveling away from home and did not have my crystal toys. Both were cleared up and gone within 3 days of coming home and using my toys.

On my next trip to Nevada, I took my two golden retrievers. The oldest dog named Perdi was about 3 years old. She had serious medical problems since birth, including severe hip dysplasia and a prolonged bout with parvo virus. My vet told me that Perdi would never survive past her fifth birthday. She was in her fourth year, and suffering from some weird disease that the vets could not identify. She had developed large growths on her paws and had lost most of her fur and much of her hair. I spent 3 weeks in Nevada during which time Perdi slept on a pad of crystal. By the time I went home she had regenerated new fur, the growths on her paws had disappeared, and she was running around like a pup. She had changed so dramatically that my teenage daughter did not recognize her when I arrived at home. She still sleeps on a crystal pad and drinks crystal water. She just turned 10, so we've doubled the vet's life expectation for her.

I have been bathing in the oil for approximately 18 months. In the first 3 months, I lost 28 pounds without exercising or changing eating habits. I've also noticed another interesting side effect. As I mentioned, I used to suffer from asthma. I also suffered from severe allergies to almost everything. I had both spring and fall hay fever seasons. Since my oil baths, I have had virtually no hay fever. I used to double-dose on two different types of hay fever medicine at least twice per day for several weeks. Since the baths, I have taken very few hay fever pills, and still have a box of pills left over from last year. I also have noticed that I need less sleep since I began taking regular oil baths. I also sleep more soundly and rarely wake up during the night.

I had a bridge in my mouth - a small tooth attached to my jaw with a metal post. It had worked its way loose and finally came out one evening. I called my dentist to arrange to have it put back in. To accommodate his schedule, I had to wait for 2 days before he could see me. I applied several drops of oil on the hole left in my mouth. This seemed to reduce the pain. When I went to see the dentist, he could not believe that the tooth could have healed itself to the extent that it had. The gums had healed completely, and the hole for the metal post was completely filled in. He thought it might be surface healing only, but upon examination, the healing extended throughout the hole area clear down to the jaw bone.

I slipped on ice and twisted my ankle. I soaked the ankle in oil twice a day for several days. I had residual pain about a month later so I went to see the doctor. X-rays showed that I had broken my ankle but the break was almost healed. Within a few weeks the pain was gone and full function returned to my ankle.

I have had several burns that have been totally healed by application of the crystal to the burned area. The burned areas should have blistered and left some sort of mark or scaring, but the areas had been totally regenerated by the next day. The crystal water also works great for sunburn.

I was recently diagnosed with a skin cancer on my cheekbone. After direct application of the oil, the skin cancer has been reduced to about one-fourth of the original size and continues to diminish with daily application of the oil."

A. P. - "I came to the Star Chamber as part of a clinical study to establish that the Experience would allow me to lose 20 pounds over a month, without dieting or any other change in lifestyle. Yes, I am losing the weight but I did not know that I was also going to get a face lift and have my vitality dynamically improved."

J. L. - "I am a 65 year old retired airline pilot. On exiting the Star Chamber I felt completely rejuvenated. It was of great interest to me, when five days later at my personal doctor's office, my blood pressure was 10 points lower on the systolic and 15 points lower on the diastolic, from where it had been for months prior to the Star Chamber Experience."

R. H. - "I was probably the first to 'fall in love' with the Star Chamber. Over the last year, I have had the experience over 250 times. I am living proof that you cannot overdo it. I really don't know what one experience will do. I do know that a complete restoration of my spine has occurred in the last year and I have x-rays to prove it. I am missing one whole person, and eat and do whatever I want. I am very strong and I don't exercise. Is it worth $300 an experience? I am 50 years old and I look, feel, act, and have clinical evidence that shows me to be a very wise 15 year old with legs and skin to die for."

C. C. - "I am the owner of a very well known health spa. My daughter had just been diagnosed as narcoleptic (a devastating inability to stay awake) before we found the Star Chamber. After three experiences she got her life back and I got my youth. This is the future and I cannot wait until we can put a Star Chamber in for our clients."

T. B. - "I'm not going to tell you how old I am,

just accept my Star Chamber Experience gave me the appearance, vitality, and strength that I had thirty years ago. It is the most lovely, soothing and wonderful experience in the world and I cannot wait to get back."

D. C. - "I am a cattle rancher, farmer, and I used to rodeo a lot. I have broken most of my ribs, a horse threw me into the fence and fell on top of me, and I broke my back years ago. I have pins in my ankle from being broken in three places. Cows have run over me from ranching. So I think you get the point. I have abused my body a lot. I am 54 years old and on top of that I got cancer 24 years ago. I have gone through years of Hell from chemotherapy and radiation treatments. I have been operated on at least 14 times from all of this. So I can really say I've been in a lot of pain.

Since I started drinking the Prill Water and soaking in the Cell Wellness Restorer, I have been relieved of so much pain and I feel so much better. It is like a Miracle. And, I really believe it makes me look younger, at least I feel younger.

Jim this Cell Wellness Restorer and Prill Water

you have developed is a blessing to mankind. I will help in anyway I can to spread the word."

L.C. - "Forty-five year old female. Weight 180 lbs. Height 5'9". I have fatigue from long hours of work and occasional back pain.

I use 2 ounces of Cell Wellness Restorer. When I soak I feel more relaxed. I am relaxed and can sleep. Reduction in pain when applied directly to tension in neck, wrists, and back. No change in digestion or elimination. Skin is softer and less wrinkled."

R. M. - "I have found that using the Prill thin water and my Barley Green, HFB and Ginkgo as well as the other juices has made me conscious that I do not need as much of the product to get the same results, which are great. It feels like I am drinking the ORIGINAL juice now. When I drink it alone, it is like it "just disappears." I can and want to drink even more water, my cells feel healthier somehow, I know that sounds strange but they do. I believe I feel younger and full of life, and people have commented on those changes to me.

One other terrific benefit is my brother, Doug. He is two years older and has a disease called Ankylosing

Spondylitis. It is an arthritic disease that, among other things, fuses your spine. His spine is almost completely fused as the last vertebrae at the top (his neck) is the only one not fused. He is a great guy with a good attitude and when you gave me some to use, I sent him some right away, in hopes it would help. Well he is feeling better every day, more relaxed, happier, and he slept on his stomach for the first time in so many years he could not remember how many years it had been. He woke up sleeping on his stomach and that very much impressed him. He had pain return to the degree he had not felt in some time, and that impressed him. He feels that could not have happened except as a result of the healing process. He is confident that if he keeps taking the baths and drinking the water, the magnesium will balance the calcium and will continue to help out his organs, and maybe even reverse the problem that caused his disease. He is excited, yes the pain excites him, as he has lived for many years with this problem and the benefits have made a believer out of him. He has dreams of being well and normal again. I am excited for him."

K. P. - "I was having a great deal of difficulty in

walking and working due to Multiple Sclerosis. I was using an electric scooter to get around at the office, since walking was so difficult. Along with that, I had very little energy and very little upper body strength, which is why I could not use a wheelchair as I could not push it with my arms. I starting using the product by pouring 2 oz. in a foot bath and soaking my feet for 10 minutes before I went to bed. After 3 days of doing this, I no longer needed the scooter at the office. I was able to walk much further and even up hills with no problems. I would like to say that the effects continued to improve but due to extreme conditions at the office, I had a relapse. I have since quit my job and am continuing the foot soak and trying bath soaks as well. I am now recovering again and am working out the routine that will work best for me. I know that I would not have done nearly as well during my relapse without the CWR1 product."

O. W. - "I am a white, retired lady, 5'6". I sprained 2 ankles, broke a toe, and arthritis tried to set in. Two ounces of the oil to painful legs relieves soreness. No problems with sleep. Skin feels softer and smoother. The oil causes a soothing, more comfortable feeling."

C. C. - "December 29, 1999 - had a glass of Thin Water - felt warmer that evening than usual (usually have a chill down the back when everyone is warm). Bath for 20 minute soak that night and felt very relaxed (ache in neck and right shoulder which I've had since a roll-over car accident 4 years ago was much better). Rubbed oil on before going to bed and had no pain in the morning. Woke up with more energy than I've had in quite awhile. I usually wake up with a headache but no headache this morning. December 30 - Drank 1 gallon of water (thin) during the day and evening. I felt like I was urinating more (kidney flush?) and felt more energy all day. Soaked my feet at night and felt great. December 31 - Bath for 20 minute soak before bedtime. Very relaxing and I felt more tired. On January 1st I had a headache (releasing toxins?) January 2 - Soaked my feet - very relaxing. Rubbed the bottom of my feet, right shoulder, and neck with oil each night and the pain has decreased and is lessened with use of my arm. Rubbed oil on a mole on my face. No noticeable results as yet. I have slept very well each night and awaken earlier and feeling more energy. I drink about 1 gallon of thin water each day. January 3 - Soaked my feet and am feeling good. No drastic changes. "

R. W. -" I am writing to thank you for the opportunity to use the Restorer Oil and the Prill thin water products. For the last two months I have been using these products, and the benefits have been calmly surprising. As you know, I am only 50 years old and in pretty good health, and aware of my well being on a daily basis. The oil has provided me with deeper rest, waking up feeling good about life. I just feel better, more relaxed, calm and I would have to say, more balanced and grounded. My energy levels have gone up, and when I had a sore back and was going to get an adjustment, I took a bath with the oil and I immediately felt better, the pain diminished and within a couple of hours, went away and I felt fine, amazing. I have found it works best for me when I take a bath in the morning, it changes my day considerably. What a way to take a supplement, just lay back and soak it up. I have also topically applied it for the supplement benefits, and when

I did, I noticed an improvement in my skin where I applied it, usually my hands and thyroid, sometimes right on my face, neck and kidney areas, especially the adrenal glands. I FIND MYSELF RECOGNIZING THAT I JUST FEEL GOOD; A SENSE OF WELL BEING THAT HAS NOT BEEN PROFOUNDLY FELT FOR SOME TIME. Thank you.

My observations from the people around me who are using the Crystal Water and the Crystal Oil are also surprising, yet in a subtle way. My mom is nearly eighty and lives next door and she has had some interesting results. She had broken her leg 4 or 5 years back and had pins put in. This caused her difficulty in walking and sleeping and since the accident, had never been able to sleep on her stomach. She is amazed that she slept deeply and comfortably for hours on her stomach, being able to roll over and not have the aches or pains she had previously. She also has had some cleansing, that is created in the healing process, and at her age the magnesium is certainly improving the use of calcium in her body. You can see it by just looking at her and others doing the same. My wife, Nancy, is no exception to that. She looks and feels better every day. The water retention she was having a problem with has disappeared and her skin is very nice. The temperament of people is changing because they are more relaxed, feeling better and I think that is a result of being able to sleep and rest so well. We are healing in our sleep, that shows that stresses are being released and we can let our body get on with what it does, maintain balance when given the proper things to help it instead of hinder it. The Crystal Oil and the Crystal Water have been wonderful additions to our lives."

K. H. - "Better overall feeling of well being. Upper respiratory improvement, better sleep, joint pain improvement, and skin irritation improvement."

C. M. - "I would rub it on any place that hurt like an old broken ankle and a sore hip or whatever before I got in the tub with it and it seemed to give relief."

J.   - "I used the CWR1 in my bath daily and I truly believe it gave me extra strength to come. One evening I didn't use it and the next morning I couldn't stay up for more than an hour at a time. I am excited about this new product."

L. H. - "I noted a reduction of aches and pains."

N. H. - "I noticed more energy."

K. C. - "I passed two kidney stones within 10 days of each other after drinking water made with Prills."

E. B. - I have noticed a deeper sleeping pattern since I have been using it. The first time I used the water in the bath. I soaked my head too and felt all sorts of movement on the inside (Positive). I then went into a cleanse that reminded me of my tears. I cleansed for nearly a week, Good. Yucky stuff from nose and throat. When this finally cleared, I noticed urinating a lot more."

T. K. - "My dry skin condition has been improved."

J. J. - "I have less soreness after playing basketball."

S. H. - "I had a severe burning backache, my husband put it on me and within minutes, it went away. This product also helped with my osteoarthritis."

M. T. - "I have been using the Kid's Magic products for about six months. I have used it to soak away tensions at the end of a hard and rigorous day. I have shared the product with friends of mine. We have all come to the same conclusion, it really helps. Besides the very nice feeling of a good night's sleep, I have also had excellent medical side effects. Recently I had a blood work up to be rated for life insurance. My rating was Preferred, and I had all better than usual for my age group. I believe this is because of the Kids Magic.

Just last week on the tennis court I popped my calf muscle and it hurt so badly that I nearly passed out. I didn't apply anything except ice throughout the first day, and I took only two Tylenol^R tablets. When I was able to bathe, I did so (this was on the second day), and then I applied the special formula of Gold, Frankincense and Myrrh. It has now been one week, and besides the soreness, and the black and blue patches on my calf and ankle, I am able to walk with virtually no pain. Something had to have done that and I believe it has been the Kid's Magic.

My friend who has been using the Magic Oil to bathe had a touch of the flu. She had a fever and just ached all over. She took a bath and within fifteen minutes the fever broke and she started to feel better.

I believe there is more to this product than just the "Placebo Effect." I am thankful to have been introduced to it and I hope it is available for the rest of my life."

T. P. - "I started using Magic Oil 6 months ago in my bath in place of epsom salt. I have a bad back, my joints hurt, I have severe muscle spasms, and sharp pains.

I really noticed the difference when I stopped using Magic Oil. The pain returned in full force. I was out of Magic Oil for two months and back on pain pills and muscle relaxers and very crabby and short tempered. Within two days of using Magic Oil again, I feel back to normal. This product is great. I know now I can't live without it. As a hair stylist for 15 years and a massage therapist in training, I have never seen a product like this with results immediately.

I feel this product aids in rebuilding osteoblasts in our bones."

J. A. - "For three years I have had an irregular patch of raised skin on my face. I felt that some day, some way, with AIM I would win this skin problem.

Well, yes! I saw my skin care specialist yesterday. She put her high-intensity light on it and said, 'Oh my gosh, I can't believe this! This is incredible! It is going away without medication.'"

J. P. - "Instead of lying awake for an hour or two when I went to bed, I began to fall asleep promptly. I slept soundly through the night. I woke up feeling rested And it was due to ᴬᴵᴹCell Wellness Restorer™."

E. S. - "I had a bad cough and achy lungs due to so much coughing. After using ᴬᴵᴹCell Wellness Restorer™ in the shower and rubbing it on my chest for a couple of days, I felt much better-the pain was gone."

K. B. - "ᴬᴵᴹCell Wellness Restorer™ was a tremendous help for my MS (multiple sclerosis) condition. I went from intense pain and walking with a cane to no pain, no swelling, and no cane."

K. H. - "I noticed results quickly. I began sleeping more deeply and felt more rested in the morning. A painful knee felt better. A rash cleared up."

R. W. - "I felt so much better. Aches and pains I had had for years disappeared. My energy returned. My hands, hands that worked in construction for years, are as soft as my wife's!"

L. S. - The last few years I have had 4 pre-
cancers burned off my face and arms. When two more
showed up on my forehead, I tried the Cell Wellness
Restorer on them and about a week and a half to two
weeks later the rough, red spots were completely gone. I
was thrilled. I also noticed a small pimple on my chin so
I dotted it also and it was gone the next morning. This
product is GREAT. Thank you AIM.

R. W. - "After using just one bottle of AIMCell
Wellness Restorer™, my psoriasis has improved
immensely. I had psoriasis over 98 percent of my body
and now I am beginning to see more skin patches and
less psoriasis patches. My skin is becoming less red and
scaly. I believe the psoriasis will be all gone soon. It's
a miracle!"

M. G. - "I rubbed AIMCell Wellness Restorer™ on
my chest and it helped clear my congestion and I slept
better."

C. C. - "This product has really been a blessing
to me. My fibromyalgia came back with a vengeance in
connection with my mother passing away. I have found

it amazing that a 20 minute soak with ^{AIM}Cell Wellness Restorer™ could make such a difference in the amount of pain I feel during the day. Without ^{AIM}Cell Wellness Restorer™, I was distracted all day long. With it, I scarcely notice the symptoms until the next morning. An added advantage - my arms and legs are now as soft as a baby's."

V. K. - "I have fibromyalgia and have tried everything. I read about ^{AIM}Cell Wellness Restorer™ in Partners and was quite skeptical but thought I'd take a chance, so I ordered one bottle. I soaked in 2 ounces and the pain in my feet and burning in my ribs went away. I also slept better than ever. I tell everyone I know about it."

J. P. - "My son, Mike, has had psoriasis since before he was a year old and he's now 40. He bathed in water with CWR added and in just one bath his psoriasis disappeared. I didn't understand at the time just why his skin cleared up and then I heard R. W. give her testimonial on the teleclass and I realized it was the CWR. If you could have seen Ruth like I have, her body covered with psoriasis, you would better understand why

CWR was such a miracle worker for her. I think CWR is going to be very good for most any skin condition. The combination of Barleygreen and CWR is a real winner."

A good friend of mine nearly cut the end of her finger off and immediately sprayed CWR on the wound. Then she soaked in her bathtub several nights and the finger has nearly healed. She would have expected good healing because of her diet and the barleygreen but she felt that even this couldn't explain the rapid healing. **Other reports that have come in from test marketing show that CWR is a potent pain reliever.** One lady got relief from rheumatoid arthritis pain in her spine and knees after using only one bottle of it. My daughter, Michelle strained her ankle. She applied CWR full strength directly to the painful area and the pain was almost instantly gone. However, it still hurt to bear weight on her ankle. That night she added CWR to her bath water and when she stepped out of the tub, her ankle no longer hurt at all. Ron, one of the owners of AIM, fell off his ladder a year ago and injured his left shoulder and it had not improved in a year's time. **By** rubbing CWR on his shoulder before he soaked in a hot tub bath with CWR in it, his shoulder pain left him.

Something very interesting are the reports from people who have multiple sclerosis. Some are walking again. Karen shared in a teleclass about her experience with multiple sclerosis. Her legs were badly swollen from her knees to her ankles and she had no feeling in her feet. Because she was unable to get in and out of the bathtub, she soaked her feet in a footbath with CWR added. **She said that the swelling in her legs is gone now and she has feeling in her feet.** She can get in and out of the tub just fine now. She was invited to speak to her multiple sclerosis support group after she had experienced such noticeable improvement.

Please note carefully how many different conditions CWR seems to help. One of my Director's husbands had a mild stroke last year. Although it left him with no deficits, he has suffered continual pain in his shoulder and arm since the stroke. Applying the CWR full strength to the painful areas has given him complete relief. This man's son has diabetic neuropathy in his

178

feet, a very painful condition. The son rubs the CWR on his feet before he goes to bed and this subdues the pain so he can sleep. Another Director had painful sciatica--she could hardly walk anymore. With the help of CWR she is experiencing her first relief from pain in a long time. The multiple sclerosis testimonials are very powerful also.

Some of the comments from those who are already using Cell Wellness Restorer as a bath additive or as a topical supplement or both. Results may vary.

☐ **Baby** "slept much better" (CWR is similar in composition to amniotic fluid). Just a half teaspoon was added to the baby's bath water each day.

☐ **Preschool children** "calmer, less hyperactivity" when bathing in it.

☐ **Athletes** reported more strength and endurance (without the dangerous side effects of steroids). One soaked his feet daily in a footbath for a year with some marvelous results.

☐ More rapid healing of **skin injuries** noted.

- **Sunburn** faded and pain gone in just a few hours after bathing in CWR and topical application.

- **Psoriasis** - reports of healing of this chronic scaling skin with CWR bath three times a week.

- **Diabetic neuropathy**..."massaged CWR into feet daily and the pain disappeared."

- **"Improved focus"**...probably related to improved sleep noted by several.

- One user reported spending $700 on medication for a **fungus infection of the toenails** over the past few months and still had the fungus. The medication was used up. She now reports that with daily baths (2 oz. CWR to tub of water) that she is growing new toenails.

- Several noted injuries such as **strained ankles**, "rubbed CWR over painful areas and experienced relief."

- Several reported **stronger fingernails**.

- An infected, **painful ingrown toenail** responded well with decreased inflammation and pain.

- **Flu and tight chest** improved when CWR was rubbed on the chest.

- Several reported **cravings** lessened and some weight loss noted.

- Several noted that **depression** improved using CWR.

- Many **restless sleepers** noted better quality of sleep and feeling more rested in the mornings.

- Two people with **severe shoulder injuries** reported noticeable improvement in comfort with daily massage of the painful area with CWR and tub bath soaks as well.

- One had sciatica for years that caused pain with every step. After bathing with CWR her pain is gone.

- **Arthritics** noted less aches and pain after rubbing directly on the affected area and bathing in it as well.

- Several with **chronic fatigue and fibromyalgia** noted much less pain.

- Someone with **bone cancer pain** reported pain relief when CWR was massaged over the painful areas.

- Someone taking **chemo** stated that "the first four

treatments made them very ill and that the treatments since using CWR have had no notable effects.

☐ Several **multiple sclerosis** patients reported improved strength and even noted being able to walk much better. They are making continued gains and are excited about this improvement.

☐ Ruth of Libby, Montana has had **severe debilitating psoriasis** for many years. Ruth has psoriasis from the top of her head to the bottoms of her feet. Psoriasis is a condition of the skin that causes it to thicken, scale, crack and bleed. In addition, she has psoriatic arthritis, a condition that sometimes accompanies psoriasis. She is wheelchair bound. She has tried everything she has ever heard of for her psoriasis but nothing has helped. She says that after using one bottle of CWR, soaking one hour three times a week, her skin experienced "massive improvement." She can see new skin growing everyday. She believes that her skin will be completely clear by the time she has used her second bottle of CWR. Praise the Lord.

"My son is a basketball player, and he is 7 foot 1 inch tall. Before he started on the Cell Restorer, he weighed 280 pounds. He now weighs 240 pounds. He looks like a lean muscle machine. He could not run up and down the basketball court twice without getting out of breath. He can now run the court the entire game and still have energy. His muscle strength has increased dramatically to the point that when he called one day, he asked what the Cell Restorer was doing to him. He said he was lifting weights and he was lifting a lot more than he was lifting the day before.

His body has changed quite a bit this past six months. The circumference of his head is more round, and his pectorals have increased. His abs look like washboards, and his coloring and skin look very healthy. In short, he looks like a very different young man. He lights up the room when he walks in. I am convinced that the Cell Restorer has made a very positive change in my son.

Everyone who has watched him play basketball cannot believe he is the same kid they watched play last year." (Author's Note: I have met this young man and his mother. He is indeed impressive. CNS)

This is Oran, the mother of the basketball player. "I would like to tell you about my experience with Cell Restorer. I'm a senior citizen. I did not know what to expect. I wasn't told anything other than it was a Cell Restorer. After about a week, my energy increased to the point where I could do all my chores the entire day and still have plenty of energy at the end of the day. (I work with horses all day.) I also was having a lot of trouble sleeping at night. I now sleep the entire night and feel very rested in the morning. My body is much more flexible. My aches and pains are gone. My skin looks ten years younger.

My husband has diabetes. His sugar levels have gone from 270 to 160. The ulcer on his leg has healed, the first time in 30 years. A large open wound on the bottom of his foot healed. It was open for one year. It healed after about four weeks. The texture of his skin on his legs has improved, it was very thin and scaly. Now it's thicker and much smoother. He has also lost weight. He has gone down three pant sizes. He also has a great deal more energy." (Author's Note: A local newspaper also carried an article about this family, including photos of a huge carrot grown from seeds soaked in Magic Water.)

During my two visits to talk with Jim and to experience the Star Chamber, I met at least half a dozen people who had benefited from their exposure. One gentleman told me that he had come off high blood pressure medications. He had had only one or two exposures in the Star Chamber but used the oil in his bath. Another man told me that his diabetes had been brought under control so that he no longer needed any diabetic medication. Then we have these written reports from numerous people, all of whom I have chosen to keep anonymous although we do have their written reports on file. The bottom line appears to be that a vast majority of those who try YINERGY™ products appear to improve in a multitude of ways. Since we know that magnesium deficiency is rampant and a basic cause of numerous disorders, that initial boost of magnesium is undoubtedly part of the answers. Longer term, we know that a majority of those who use the products in adequate quantity have a restoration of DHEA, another big boost to Life Energy. Although it may take us many years to determine other scientific reasons for benefit from YINERGY™ products, we now know that thousands have used them with no significant problem and most have benefited. Obviously, as with any medical problem, you should always integrate any self-care with appropriate medical advice.

CHAPTER 8

THE AGE OF AQUARIUS

THIS IS THE AGE OF AQUARIUS: The Age of
Aquarius, the sign of the water bearer, has been
prophesized for decades to bring about great change and
good change. YINERGY™ Water and Oil is being
released to the world just after the Grand Conjunction of
early May 2000, the "official beginning of the Aquarian
Age" according to some.

Other than air, water is the most essential
requirement for human life. It is conceivable that both
Jim Carter and John Hamaker are correct. Jim's story
you know. Almost two decades ago, John Hamaker in
THE SURVIVAL OF CIVILIZATION warned of the
catastrophic problems of demineralization of soil. He
found that pulverized *glacial* rock rejuvenated plant life
with no other "fertilizer." It is well known that
historically, for millions of years, the cycle of glaciation
and non-glaciation has proceeded, 100,000 years of
glaciation to 10,000 years of non-glaciation.

Jim has emphasized the importance of glacial water. It appears that during the 100,000 years of glaciation, the mica-like laminar crystal he believes came from space, might be stored and available to rejuvenate the earth when glaciers melt. Most of that storage will eventually be at the bottom of the oceans. Remember that 1 gallon of sea water contains 6 oz. of the oil. Great storage will also occur at some earth spots such as that which creates the San Juan effect. I have not had the privilege of testing pure glacial water as I have Magic Water and Magic Oil. But my simple physical tests prove that this is a *very unique form of water*!

UNIQUE WATER

There are a number of unusual characteristics of the YINERGY™ products. Cell Wellness Restorer or Magic Oil has a pH of 4.5 and a specific gravity of greater than 1.30. Obviously it would sink to the bottom of the ocean! Regular water has a pH of 7 and a specific gravity of 1.000. When I use one of our regular chem sticks, the kind we would use to check urine in patients, it is extremely positive for nitrite and for blood! Even at dilutions of 25 parts water to 1 part of the oil, there is still a positive test for nitrite and the specific gravity is still greater than 1.025 but the pH has now gone up to 9 or above.

Water made from a combination of the Laminar Crystals and the Prills has a pH of 9. One of the great enigmas of this material is how can an acid (negative charge) be converted into a basic (positive charge) liquid substance only with the addition of water? Chemical analyses by a variety of labs have also given some unusual facts. In one test, Prill Water started at a pH of 5.8 but 24 hours later had a pH of 10.7. Regular filtered water required 10 mg. of baking soda to raise its pH to 8.8. The crystals in the Magic Oil when analyzed separately contained ammonium magnesium chloride. That would account for the positive nitrates that I found on testing. The iron might account for the positive test for blood.

Another test of the oil revealed per 100 grams.

Total Crude Fat, grams   0.05

Total Crude Protein, grams 0.26

Total Moisture, grams   51.31

Ash (mineral matter) grams 19.09

Other, grams	29.29	
Rubidium, grams	0.43	23 parts/ml
Strontium, grams	2.71	142 parts/ml
Manganese, mg.	1.58	88 parts/ml
Copper, mg.	0.23	12 parts/ml
Iron, mg.	2.52	32 parts/ml
Zinc, mg.	0.15	8 parts/ml
Magnesium, grams	7.70	40.38%
Chloride, grams	4.25	22.33%
Calcium, grams	1.75	9.16%
Potassium, grams	0.11	0.57%

In a separate test lab using x-ray fluorescence analysis came up with:

Iron	0.23%
Magnesium	61.86%
Silicone	0.24%
Calcium	0.45%
Strontium	10 parts/ml
Arsenic	18 parts/ml
Manganese	500 parts/ml
Cooper	8 parts/ml
Zinc	41 parts/ml

The Prills themselves when analyzed for composition gave total metals in parts per million:

Magnesium		628,000
Calcium		3,650
Arsenic		0.98
Lead		0.25
Copper		4.37
Zinc		45
Iron		1,500
Mercury	Less than	0.0100
Cadmium		0.84
Manganese		8.36
Strontium		11.13
Silicon		1.880

The FDA guideline for cadmium is less than 55 micrograms per day. A person would have to consume 4.17 liters of the Prills themselves to exceed the FDA level.

The Prills themselves were found to have a pH of 11.52 and to be essentially free of organisms.

Prill Water was found to have essentially no

sodium, potassium or iron but to have 5.13 parts/million of calcium and 176 parts/million of magnesium with a pH of 9.98 and a total alkalinity of 240.

These unusual chemical aspects may not have much meaning to you but Jim Carter believes that there are three energies in our biosphere. He believes that blue light originates from the sun and is sunlight itself. He believes that red is the electricity produced by the dynamo effect of the earth and that yellow is spatial, a matter of space drawn by the rotation of the earth.

THE ESOTERIC TECHNICAL

as presented by Jim Carter

Twenty five years ago I was given an artifact that is a demonstration of a unique system of energy handling. In a situation where everything is in motion, the ability to achieve "stillness" is power.

My diagram of the energy handling system of the artifact - STONE.

5   4   3   2   1   (6)   7   8

Blue   .   .   .   .   Yellow   Red

.   .   .   .   .   (Source)   .

.   Natural Negative   Man Made   .

.   .   Electricity   .   .   Electricity   .

Sun   .   (H^2O)   Man Made

Light Recognized   Water   .   Materials

Life   (Vital Fluid)   .

Laminar Crystal

In its simplest, this is the diagram of a "teeter totter" with 6 being the fulcrum point. The numbers can be taken as units of weight and it can be readily seen that there is the same amount of weight on each side, 15. The micro-effects of the board of this "teeter totter" is relative to the conventional power applications of the world. The Macro is the balance in the world itself.

The artifact is a demonstration of a small "teeter totter" where only the aspect of the crystal, or 1, and that of a man made stone, or 7, are of issue. When this stone

193

is brought into "near perfect balance" it becomes an accumulator of negative electricity. The stone was balanced and controlled by the mind of the operator.

This generation of power can be seen as a damming effect, that causes a slowing in the flow of the Source energy and the electricity accumulated is the first "natural attempt" to restore this flow to its proper uninterrupted condition. The diagram shows a perfect balance between natural and man-made materials. The slowing of the primal flow on a macro-level is near if not already taking place. This is indicated by accumulations of electricity, causing hot and cold spots, and of course weather changes.

Our conflict with this flow is unacceptable on a cosmic level. We could be very close to understanding what it means to dam the act that is the source of all life. We did this successfully for an instant, and called it a nuclear explosion.

Cell Wellness Restorer, Magic Oil or YINERGY™ Oil is a unique substance that appears to be what Jim calls "Phase Formed Water." It clearly has a different *structure* from "ordinary" water. It has been used both internally and externally, although, I have to say I haven't taken it internally yet. It has been used everywhere on the surface of the body but does cause a stinging sensation on the face and on the external genitalia and in very sensitive individuals, of the feet. In its pure undiluted form, the oil may cause redness of the skin in a small percentage of people. Jim reports that washing the area with soap and water prior to applying the oil prevents stinging. And, of course, washing it off with water will eliminate the stinging very rapidly. A topical application of the oil directly to the body is one of the best ways to get a maximum amount of the oil absorbed through the skin. For those who do not like the slight stinging aspects that may occur with the undiluted oil, mixing it 50/50 with water and spraying it on the body is another way of excellent rapid absorption.

Magic Oil, Cell Wellness Restorer™, or YINERGY™ Oil can also be used in the bath with from 2 oz. to 32 oz. having been studied in a regular bathtub.

Magic Water or Prill Water also appears to be different from regular water. If you spray it on the skin, the skin feels as if there is a fine layer of wax on it after the water dries. It certainly can be drunk and I have drunk as much as 2 quarts of water per day.

Sea Snow should be made into a paste with Magic Water or Prill Water and applied to any area as a "mask." This is allowed to dry and then is washed off with regular water. It is a fine cleanser of skin

Snow Crystal is a fine brown powder which seems to come from melting snow at very high elevations. It can actually be buffed into the skin with a dry cloth and converts water in the skin directly into Magic Water.

Magic Drops are a highly purified version of Magic Oil being approximately 25% magnesium chloride. This is one of the ways of restoring magnesium to the 70+% of all individuals who are deficient in magnesium. It does have a very strong salty and somewhat bitter taste.

At the very least, everyone can benefit from drinking the water and spraying it on the skin, as well as using the oil directly on the skin or in a bath.

"MAGIC WATER"

(The Vital Fluid)

This liquid is produced in nature by the contact of common water with the halo effect of any structure that concentrates the energy that is loosely called "Life Force." Depending upon the purity of this contact, the water molecule is altered. Slight impact produces a shrinking of the water molecule resulting in the substance known as "deuterium oxide" or "heavy water." Stronger impacts result in a cold fusion of the hydrogen atoms of the water molecule, producing a new atomic substance - "Vital Fluid."

Vital fluid is extremely similar to common water in many of its characteristics. This had made isolation or separation virtually impossible, resulting in the erroneous conclusion that common water was responsible for the moisture in living tissue. The single strongest indicator that there was something "other than common water" involved in cellular moisture comes from the moisturizing effects of plant juices such as aloe vera.

The attempts to recreate the restorative effects of plant juices has led to the use of surfactants which alter

197

the surface tension of common water, resulting in the absorption and thus "hydration" of cells. There is a huge difference between "restoring the moisture" of a cell and "flooding it with common water or hydration." This difference is dynamically demonstrated by the fact that "vital fluid" restores the life to burned cells, while surfacted common water destroys them.

A reasonable analogy of what takes place can be drawn by using a basketball as an example. If this ball is perfectly inflated, it has wonderful and controllable dynamics. The vital fluid works with the cells to produce perfect spherical formation and thus perfect dynamics. Over-inflation of the basketball results in the same consequences as are found with surfacted water hydration in cells and under-inflation is called "dehydration," the results of which are commonly known.

The property of cells that are perfectly round and dynamic is seen as youth. In the skin these dynamics are seen as "tightness or resilience" and a shine that reflects energies that are consistent with good health, resulting in the pink or rosy color. In the muscle and soft tissue, these same dynamics are represented by "tone and strength." The success of any living system is dependent upon good cellular dynamics.

The magic of "Magic Water" is in the fact that nature produces it as the beginning of proliferation. It is the key ingredient in embryonic fluid, and constituents. Restoring this liquid stasis is restoring youth.

"MAGIC OIL"
(Phase II Vital Fluid or Vital Oil)

The energy that produces "vital fluid" is capable of further alteration of this liquid into a more concentrated state. This is an "oil-like" inorganic substance that is the key aspect in most plant saps and seeds. Again, since this oil is "so similar" to hydrocarbon oils, it has gone without recognition.

Because the skin is intelligent and because it will absorb the "Vital Fluid" and other forms, i.e. oils and waxes, it could be said that the human body was designed to seek out these primary substances. Since they are all simply forms of the same thing, the body is capable of conversion of one form into another for its specific purposes. It would be very easy to draw a

199

picture of a living entity that was made entirely of "forms of water."

We say that the "Magic Water" is for the skin, and the "Magic Oil" is for soft tissue, cartilage and bone. This inorganic oil can take on a number of different forms. It can be returned to the "fine liquid state of Vital Fluid" or further reduced to the consistency of a resin. It is the primary ingredient in cartilage and the binder in bone, as well as the key ingredient of digestive juices. Thus, it could be said that "a shortage of this substance" is directly related to changes in life.

People are made of a somewhat convoluted mixture of "Vital Fluid" and "Vital Oil," and mineral and hydrocarbon stuff. We have subjectively proven that a shortage of this oil is responsible for the failure of life during gestation. Being born with a shortage of this oil is likely responsible for the phenomenon known as "crib death" as well as most degenerative diseases during childhood and adolescence. It is decidedly related to the change in life called "adulthood" and this is proven by the almost immediate, degradation of the bone that begins, noticeably, just after adulthood is reached.

Adulthood is caused by a shortage of "Vital Oil." Because digestion is far more important than bone strength, the body begins robbing the bone for this oil to maintain digestion. By the time we reach 40 to 50 years of age the reserve in the bone is depleted to a point where another phenomenon takes place. This time we begin to show rapid degradation, caused by a failing digestive system. The supplementation of this "Vital Oil" will arrest the aging process. A little slows it. More stops it, and enough will reverse it. This is what we call "Magic Oil" or "Vital Oil." Mothers who have oil supplementation will make strong healthy babies. Children who have this supplementation may never have to grow old. Aged people who have oil supplementation can regain their youth. Unfortunately, it will be many years before people come to respect that this is TRUE.

REPORTED USES OF YINERGY™ PRODUCTS
MAGIC WATER - THE ULTIMATE

1. To restore the moisture to the skin, particularly of the face
2. To remedy dry eyes and itchy eyes.
3. To refresh, when tired. Spray it on the face.

4. For dry or chapped lips.

5. To soothe irritated lungs, inhale the mist.

6. In place of a deodorant.

7. As a remedy for yeast infection.

8. A preventative and treatment for diaper rash.

9. A remedy for poison ivy or poison oak.

10. Instant relief and restoration for burns.

11. Treatment of bug bites.

12. Treatment of scrapes and abrasions.

13. Instant relief of pain and restoration of sun burn.

14. Relief of itching

Dehydration is the single largest issue in appearance and comfort. Magic Water moisturizes, which is the answer to dehydration.

MAGIC OIL - FOR RESTORATION

1. Treatment for osteoporosis.

2. Restoration of cartilage in joints.

3. Promotes healing.

4. Used in place of soap, and shampoo - restores hair color.

5. Improves sexual performance and enhances attributes.

6. Tones, softens and strengthens skin. A treatment for all bad conditions.

7. Repels negative environmental energies.

8. Restores primary energy - Life Force Energy - conductivity.

9. Used as a disinfectant.

10. As a treatment for bites and stings.

11. Treatment of back pain.

12. Treatment of joint pain.

13. Treatment of arthritis and rheumatism.

14. Treatment of tennis elbow and carpal tunnel syndrome.

15. Enhances digestion.

16. Treatment for sprains, bumps and bruises.

17. Enhances physical strength.

18. Removes age spots.

19. Restores scar tissue and stretch marks.

20. Relieves stress.

Concentrated Magic Oil is a mild mineral acid. On dilution with common water it becomes absolutely neutral and on further dilution it becomes alkaline.

Magic Oil is an extremely rapid healant. If you use it

straight, be prepared for this rapid action. It is not an irritant.

"PHYSICAL RESTORATION"
(Cleaning House So That The Energy Can Flow)

In the early days of medicine, most disease was qualified as CONGESTION. Literally this means that systems were inhibited from proper function. The remedy, treatment and cure was some manner of decongestant. During this stage of medical development, many of the top researchers were quoted as saying that "the human body was capable of a very long functional life, if the cause of this congestion could be found," further stating that "750 to 1000 years would be reasonable."

Congestion is an issue of great concern. If we take the sum total of the materials of a human body, we find that it is virtually all liquid, generally assumed to be water. The percentage of minerals and carbon would be consistent with "very good water" if it was observed as a contaminant. It is the study of "how to build a human system out of its contamination" that has led to all the confusion. It is fair to assume that contamination causes congestion and thus slows restoration even if the proper materials for this restoration are available.

Following the lead of the best current observers, "simple sugars" may be the greatest contributors to the congestion of the body functions. Simple sugars are in fact made of "common water," while their complex counterparts are "at least largely based on vital fluid." One product of simple sugars is "starches" and starches are resistant to the most common cleaning mechanism of the body. Simple sugars are ionized into forms that travel into the "most protected" areas of the body and are reduced by STRESS in these sanctuaries into starches.

This results in congestion of primary organs, perhaps the third brain or Medulla Oblongata, which with the hypothalamus controls the entire involuntary function of the body. Since the enzyme "pancreatin" is the primary defense against this "starch congestion"; and since failure of the organ that produces pancreatin causes a disease called "sugar diabetes" and since this disease is only partially treated, to prevent insulin shock, we have a huge example of the congestive damage of starch in the degradation of diabetics. Even more, the fact that pancreatin is too large a molecule to enter the third brain, we should assume that "starch congestion" in this organ is largely without natural remedy so long as the body is deficient in "Vital Fluid."

There is a degradation of starch caused by contact with "Vital Fluid," a sublingual preparation that Jim Carter believes cleanses congestion from the Medulla Oblongata. He calls this "Magic Drops" and it has been used as a symptomatic or a tonic with remarkable success. These drops are a mixture of "Magic Oil" and "Magic Water" and by placing them directly in the mouth for instant absorption, some rapid action can be achieved.

In other locations, where the blood flow has been restricted by congestion another mechanism is brought into play. This substance is called "Sea Snow." It is produced by placing the "Magic Oil" in a strong positive field and literally moving it away from its perfection. This produces a substance with an extremely high affinity for congestive materials that bypasses the barrier of the skin. This interface allows congestive materials to be pulled directly from soft tissue through the skin without any disruption of the integrity of the skin cells. There is no real certainty as to why this works; the proof that it does is in the use.

Finally, there are "Snow Crystals" which is the phase of vital fluid produced by the impact of Life Force energy on frozen water, on snow. The reason for the use of this product lies in the fact that it is an accumulator of Life Force energy. This accumulation can alter the water that is trapped in cells restoring the "Vital Fluid" by contact rather than replacement.

In our world today, we have a few examples of cultures of people who live nearly twice as long as normal. These people have one thing in common that is representative of our position. They all have "glacial water" sources, and glacial water has a high percentage of "Vital Fluid." These people live in the most hostile environments in the world and yet live longer than in civilization! When the percentage of "Vital Fluid" in common water reaches a ratio of about 1 part vital fluid to 300 parts of water, the water appears blue. With an increase of vital fluid it will be deep blue, eventually reaching a concentration where the color again returns to clear.

Plant juices have a higher percentage of vital fluid because cellulose is a concentrator of Life Force energy. Plants that are perennial continue to impact water into its "vital fluid stage" and then into its "vital oil" phase. Plant oils are generally loaded with hydrocarbons to be ingested without discomfort. The application to the skin does however achieve the same result as the "Magic Oil" as is seen in the use of flax and other organic seed oils.

The objective of this whole event is the presentation of a scenario that will cause people to "make available" the BUILDING BLOCKS OF LIFE both to their own bodies and those of their children. Unfortunately, presenting a fact is not necessarily a suitable motivation to generate an action. Presenting a reason, is usually a much better motivator.

"RETURNING TO THE FLOW"
(What is Life Force Energy?)

Jim believes that "life was designed" to be totally constructed of the "first water" referenced in the Book of Genesis. This water originated by the design of the Creator from the Void, which he considers to be SPACE. It has been proven that the impedance or frequency of space is exactly the same as the energy accumulated at the apex of right angles. The substance of the right angle does not really seem to be the issue, just that the shape is such an angle. Thus, "the energy that animates life is the energy represented by the void or emptiness of space."

All energies have many forms. Sunlight for instance, materializes through the plant kingdom as carbon. Positive electricity produces a solid phase that has recently become known as "free radicals." The energy of space materializes as a vital fluid that has been long called water - the water of life to be exact. For our purposes, we don't need to go beyond the first water, because the forms that nature generates are very adequate to provide all the parts and pieces for humans. There are fluid, oil, wax, and solid flexible materials that all correspond to the impedance of space.

The Prime Objective is to return to consistency with the energy that animates life. This can only be accomplished by returning to the materials that are consistent with this flow.

What experiments, both by Jim and me, have shown and continue to show is that "regardless of the condition" of the physical body, it is capable of reorganizing itself with these materials, if they are made available. There is nothing broken until the system quits and even then, it might be restored to function if it is not digested by some other life form. Remember the mummies!

Imagine if you will, a "water-like" being, with the ability to reshape and reorganize itself by its own will. Even more, a being that has the ability to reshape the matter around it into any desired shape. This is not the power of Creation, but it is a power that denies dominion by one person over another. Holding a race of such beings hostage has required their ignorance of their potential. Endless lies have compounded themselves into a mass illusion that can only be explained as a mystery. The rules are changing.

The stone referred to in the beginning of this book was much like a Rosetta Stone that allowed the understanding of ancient languages. Jim's stone may be the Rosetta Stone of Water and it has allowed the understanding of a third energy that is as real as electricity or the light from the Sun, yet totally distinct from either. This energy appears to be spatial in origin, the matter of the Void of Space. Our understanding is continually expanding and growing but has a long way to go!

The Crystal technology has to do with a unique laminar crystal that is the active agent in the ancient stone and an accumulator of this third energy. This Crystal has evolved into what Jim calls the Star Chamber. Loosely called two naps and a bath, the Star Chamber is a system designed to return the character of youth. Five products have been designed to reinforce the health improvements of those who experience the Star Chamber. Two of them, Magic Oil and Magic Water, worked so well even without the Star Chamber experience, that it was important that people and especially their children have them, thus, "Kid's Magic." If you haven't taken a bath with a couple of ounces of Magic oil or sprayed Magic Water on your face, you are simply missing a great treat. Reversing the aging process is a miracle. Young individuals who use YINERGY™ products may never need the Star Chamber if they simply take an occasional bath with Magic Oil, but for those of us who have achieved adulthood, the Star Chamber may be a major assistant in restoring youth.

THE STAR CHAMBER:
TWO NAPS AND A BATH

The first nap is simply resting on a bed made of millions of Natural black crystals that have the unique character of accumulating and donating only negative electricity. This form of electricity is compatible with life. FACT: The positive end of a compass needle is attracted to each point of this crystal; thus, the crystal only produces negative electricity. The objective of this bed is to place a person in a huge Negative Mass Action Effect, with the intent of balancing or softening the positive electricity in the system - to bring it back into a water soluble form. In its simplest context, the term "free radical" is just positive electricity, and some of the best scientists in the world have said that, when there is enough positive electricity in one space at one time, it transforms into solids: thus, the importance of the Black Crystal Bed. This is the principle of antioxidant times millions.

The bath is next. This consists of soaking for

about 20 minutes in 135 gallons of Magic Water, accompanied by an appropriate amount of Magic Oil. Magic Water restores the moisture on a cellular level, while the Magic Oil restores the cell walls. Magic Water is made by saturating the common water molecule with the energy of the Crystal - driving out all its electricity. Magic Oil can be made by placing Magic Water in a strong vacuum or it can be extracted from sea water and then treated with the Crystal to remove absorbed electricity.

Unlike common water, Magic Water appears to be absorbed rapidly by the skin - the skin accepts it, and loves it. It fills cells to their best, most dynamic, inflation and when the cell is full, the excess is no longer taken in, thus, delivering perfect moisturization. As the Magic Water is absorbed, common water, which is a tremendous solvent, is expelled as perspiration, carrying with it all manner of impurities, including positive electricity. This cellular laundering is massive, with perhaps an absorption of five to seven gallons of Magic Water in twenty minutes. Of course this means that an equal amount of common water is expelled. Logically, if you do not remove the toxic materials from your body, changing their form with antioxidants or any other chemical, natural or synthetic, will simply alter the symptoms. The Star Chamber bath appears to purify the water of your body.

Magic Water is the vital liquid found in embryonic fluid and the other liquids of the body that are scientifically called fluids. We know this now because we have synthesized this liquid and developed standards so that we can measure the percentages of this vital liquid in complex substances. The amounts of this vital liquid, i.e. Magic Water, is directly related to the beneficial qualities of Aloe Vera, and fruit and vegetable juices. Proper distillation of Aloe Vera proves that the "magic of the burn plant" is in its water alone, its Magic Water. We have not proven this yet, but it may be that the power of herbs, essential oils, even minerals and their oils can be equated directly to a single oily substance, a Magic Oil. The crossing of effects, the ability of many oily substances to achieve the same result would lend itself to their being a common denominator, a truly ESSENTIAL OIL. We call this Magic Oil. Magic Oil, for example, has the same effect as essential oils when it is used a few drops at a time but since it costs less than $2.00 an ounce, instead of the $20.00 an ounce you might pay for the best Lavender oil, you can use a lot more. You can experience what would happen if you put two ounces of an essential oil in your bath, simply by putting a few drops of any essential oil in the Magic Oil and then adding it to your bath. If you want to go to the efforts to have a blood chemistry baseline done before and after you do this, you will see that there are huge changes within a month. We use essential oils to direct the effect of Magic Oil and because we like the way they smell.

The Magic Oil part of this bath appears to be that of a powerful restoration of cells. It returns the strength of cells and thus their dynamics and vitality. Depending on the individual, the amount of Magic Oil ranges from a couple of ounces to a gallon. There are no side effects or counter indications, SAVE BECOMING YOUNGER. Magic Oil is only life positive, and your body knows exactly what to do with it.

After the bath, there is another nap. This time it

is in the accumulated energy of the Crystal itself. If the human body is a biological battery, as we believe and many scientists agree, then there must be a source of charging energy. When the potential of food is properly established, it becomes clear that we do not get enough energy from our food to account for the work force expended by the body. Perhaps this is why Christ said that we do not live by bread alone. At any rate, it simply does not add up. We must have an external charging source, and we must plug into it when our bodies are at rest. The energy of the Crystal appears to be that source so the third aspect of the Star Chamber is bringing the human biological battery back to FULL CHARGE. This is rapidly accomplished when the volume of this energy exceeds the normal levels found in our environment. Today, everyone knows what happens to batteries that are operated at partial charge - they fail. The idea of the Crystal Bed is to saturate the entire body with Life Force Energy, driving out other energies, like electricity, and returning it to the fully charged character of youth. The proof that this works is in the huge increase in vitality and usable energy experienced by those who go through the Star Chamber system. It is also apparent in any exhausted person who simply lies down on this bed for a few minutes.

The Baby Star Chamber is by no means perfect. it is a lot of work and has some serious limitations as to the number of people that it can accommodate but 150 people have experienced it, including me. Indeed, I am so impressed that I hope to add a "Star Chamber" to my already world renowned clinic, the Shealy Wellness Center.

In the 21st Century, treatment of disease may be two naps and a bath, instead of surgery and chemotherapy. It will be this way because it is much more profitable for the HMO's. The primary disease that afflicts mankind will be declared to be DESTRUCTIVE AGING and the remedy to all its symptoms, particularly what is presently called degenerative diseases will be to BECOME YOUNGER.

MIST MAGIC™

(The "Future" in Produce Management
and Stabilization)

Mist Magic is a simply applied unit that changes the character of the water in the misting system used to maintain the moisture in lettuce and other perishable produce. In most cases it is only a matter of cutting the water line in the existing misting system and connecting them so that the water passes through the Mist Magic Unit.

The shelf life of high perishable produce is directly related to oxidation and to parasitic growth that rapidly attacks the area burnt by atmosphere. Mist Magic changes the character of water by contact. Nothing is added or taken away from the water. Water that is altered in this fashion has a much higher absorption rate that prevents dehydration and thus oxidation. It even appears to restore wilted leaves after the fact. This system taps into a natural energy that is unique to our technology. It is not magnetic, chemical, and requires no outside power source. Hopefully it will be available within the next year.

THE NEXT GENERATION OF
THE STAR CHAMBER

It begins with a lens shaped pool, about 150 feet in diameter. Tapering from its edge to a center depth of twelve feet. This pool is made of a mixture of "The Crystal" and "reconstituted limestone." In the center of this large pool is a second smaller pool, about 50 feet in diameter. This pool is made of a permeable ceramic with "The Crystal." The large pool is a "hydrogen recombiner" producing an altered water - a heavier smaller molecule that will pass through the ceramic barrier, presenting a highly concentrated version of "altered water" in the center pool. This water is extremely pure, as the altered molecule does not have the chelation ability of its precursor. It is also the perfect hydrant for the human skin.

Around the large pool is a common walkway about fifteen feet wide. There are three bridges, connecting this walkway to the walkway around the center pool, which is about eight feet wide. The bridges flow from the main walkway, starting at about ten feet wide and flowing into the center walkway at about six feet wide. Circles in circles.

The pool area is covered by a geodesic dome made of metal and "gold filmed glass" creating an atmosphere that is a "yellow green twilight" in the daytime. The dome is lit at night through "gold film" maintaining the same effect. The dome has a "planetarium correct" star-scape that presents a perfect, starry sky when the internal lights are dimmed. The same "glow in the dark material" is used to mark walkways and provide light for the people using the chamber at night.

Surrounding the "Star Chamber" are twenty-four apartments. Each apartment has direct access to the chamber and a second entrance into a basement level. There is a third, patio exit into the glassed in "garden area" that surrounds the complex. The apartments are three levels, providing enclosing parking, living and sleeping areas. The apartment complex is square with the eight apartments on each side. The corners are dedicated to other activities relating to the program. The apartments are designed to present an environment that is about half way between the "Star Chamber" and the world. The surrounding garden is a "deep woods effect." The "Star Chamber" effect is a virtual cessation of pain on a cellular level which people will need to be able to "get away from" if it becomes too intense.

Three of the corner areas must be dedicated to the three aspects of the "Star Chamber Experience." The fourth corner should be a theater effect, for meetings, educational services and recreation and dining.

CORNER AREA ONE is the "negative ion effect." The objective of this area is to place people, individually, in a massive negative energy field. This is to soften the "free radicals" and present them in a water soluble form.

CORNER AREA TWO is the "Prill Bath" which is designed to launder the inert water of the system through the skin. This is a physical transference of "altered water" into the body and "charged or polluted water" out as perspiration. This removes hard water, water that is polluted with hydrocarbons and water that has combined with hydrogen (acids), replacing it with

221

extremely pure, "non-polar" water. The only chemical used in the "Star Chamber" is WATER. Cleaning the cellular water, immediately starts the restoration process of the skin, and tight skin with good color is the aspect that most people would agree to be the "appearance of Youth." The baths themselves are glass lined, silver plated lens shaped, double boilers, each with its own temperature control.

CORNER AREA THREE is dedicated to bringing the "human biological battery" back to its "full charge potential." This is an area of small "Star Chamber" and Crystal Beds. The third phase of the Star Chamber Experience is resting on the Crystal.

These three aspects represent one hour per day for the users. Other physical therapy could be incorporated into this system, although the system exceeds "all other physical therapy" combined. There is no intent of offering any special services beyond the Crystal effects. This system does not require any lifestyle changes on the part of the participant.

The program is to be used by those participating "one week" every six months. Beyond this week of resting, relaxing, and restoring, these people will be provided with their own "Crystal Sleeper" for home use. The intent of this device is to maintain the "full charge characteristic" of the newly restored "human biological battery."

There are any number of additions that can be offered to those who want them ranging from ongoing supplementation of their "body water" to home conversions to present a much less detrimental "home environment." This technology can spin off into virtually every aspect of human endeavor.

The object of the "one week" event is to "turn back the biological clock by twenty years. In the case of those who don't have twenty years of age to give up, they will return to their best point. Children who have this experience simply "become awesome."

THE SECRET OF HEALTHY LIFE

I have not included in this book my usual comments about the effects of stress or my usual recommendations for no smoking, optimal nutrition, physical exercise and relaxation. All of these are great tools for optimizing health. All of them require some degree of WILL POWER and motivation. True "couch potatoes" are not likely to be pushed into action by any comments I might make. But *maybe* they will use the bath, with YINERGY™ Oil, as a couch substitute.

To start, they should not exceed 105°F and perhaps 5 to 10 minutes. I like 108°F and 30 minutes.

My resting pulse is 60. After this rejuvenating, re-energizing bath, my pulse is 152, two and a half times resting pulse. Pulse-wise, this is equal to that which I can achieve with a brisk jog! Although it won't build muscle strength in my arms and legs, it obviously exercises my heart! And there is great evidence that both prostaglandin E1 and beta endorphins are increased by heat. Prostaglandin E1, beta endorphin, heart exercise, marvelous relaxation - plus increased magnesium and DHEA! And, almost no effort. This combination cannot be beaten - or equaled with any other known approach. *Combined they may well be the Fountain of Youth.*

THIS IS THE AGE OF AQUARIUS, the beginning of a new millennium with the potential for enhancing life and health. The "simple" fact that YINERGY™, Cell Wellness Restorer™, and Magic Oil raise DHEA and intracellular magnesium makes it the *single most potent* substance I know. There is no drug, no *single* other treatment known that has the potential to prevent and/or reverse the numerous illnesses associated with magnesium and DHEA depletion. Couple those with the benefits of heat, heart exercise and relaxation. Ponce de Leon rejoice: These do present us with the Secret of a Good and Healthy Life, HOLY WATER, SACRED OIL, THE FOUNTAIN OF YOUTH.

DHEA REFERENCE SOURCES

1. Connor, Elizabeth Barret; Khaw, Kay-Tee; and Yen, Samuel. "A Prospective Study of Dehydroepiandrosterone Sulfate, Mortality, and Cardiovascular Disease." The New England Journal of Medicine, 1986; 315(24):1519-1524.

2. Dilman, V.M. "Pathogenetic Approaches to Prevention of Age-Associated Increase of Cancer Incidence." Annals New York Academy of Sciences, 1991; 621:385-400.

3. De La Torre, B.; Fransson, J.; Scheynius, A. "Blood Dehydroepiandrosterone Sulphate (DHEAS) Levels in Pemphigoid/Pemphigus and Psoriasis. Clinical and Experimental Rheumatology, 1995; 13:345-348.

4. Gordon, G.B.; Helzlsouer, K.J.; Comstock, G.W. "Serum Levels of Dehydroepiandrosterone and Its Sulfate and the Risk of Developing Bladder Cancer. Cancer Research 1991; 51(5):1366-13669.

5. Ivanovic, S.; Agbaba, D.; Zivanov-Stakie, D.;
    Konstantinovic, I. "The Urinary
    Dehydroepiandrosterone, Androsterone and
    Etiocholanolone Excretion of Healthy Woman and
    Women with Benign and Malignant Breast
    Disease." Journal of Clinical Pharmacy and
    Therapeutics, 1990; 15:213-219.

6. Mitchell, Laura E.; Sprecher, Dennis L.; Borecki,
    Ingrid B.; Rice, Treva; Laskarzewski, Peter M.;
    and Rao, D. C. "Evidence for an Association
    Between Dehydroepiandrosterone Sulfate and
    Nonfatal, Premature Myocardial Infarction in
    Males." Circulation, 1994; 89(1):89-93

7. Mortola, J.F., and Yen, S.S.C. "The Effects of
    Oral Dehydroepiandrosterone on Endocrine-
    Metabolic Parameters in Postmenopausal
    Women." Journal of Clinical Endocrinology and
    Metabolism, 1990; 71(3):696-704.

227

8. Nestler, John E.; Usiskin, Keith S.; Barlascini, Cornelius O.; Welty, Devin F.; Clore, John N.; and Blackard, William G. "Suppression of Serum Dehydroepiandrosterone Sulfate Levels by Insulin: An Evaluation of Possible Mechanisms." Journal of Clinical Endocrinology and Metabolism, 1989; 69(5):1040-1046.

9. New York Academy of Sciences. "Dehydroepiandrosterone (DHEA) and Aging. Abstracts from June 17-19, 1995 meeting.

10. Regelson, William; Loria, Roger; and Kalimi, Mohammed. "Hormonal Intervention: "Buffer Hormones" or "State Dependency." Annals New York Academy of Sciences, 1988; 521:260-273.

11. Rosch, Paul. "DHEA and the Fountain of Youth." The Newsletter of the American Institute of Stress, 1995; 8:1-3.

12. Shealy, C. Norman. "DHEA - THE YOUTH AND HEALTH HORMONE." Keats Publishing, Inc., New Canaan, Connecticut, 1996.

13. Shealy, C. Norman. "A Review of Dehydroepiandrosterone (DHEA). Integrative Physiological and Behavioral Science, 1995; 30(4):304-309.

14. Shealy, C. Norman; Myss, Caroline M.; Cady, Roger K.; Dudley, Lucia; and Cox, Richard H. "Electrical Stimulation Raises DHEA and Improves Diabetic Neuropathy." Stress Medicine 1995; 11:215-217.

15. Shealy, C. Norman and Myss, Caroline M. "The Ring of Fire and DHEA: A Theory for Energetic Restoration of Adrenal Reserves." Subtle Energies, 1995; 6(2):168-175.

16. Stahl, F.; Schnorr, D.; Pilz, C.; and Dorner, G. "Dehydroepiandrosterone (DHEA) Levels in Patients with Prostatic Cancer, Heart Diseases and Under Surgery Stress." Experimental and Clinical Endocrinology, 1992; 99(2):68-70.

17. USA Today, September 5, 1996. "DHEA: Is This Hormone the Fountain of Youth?"

18.   Williams, Daniel P.; Boyden, Thomas W.; Pamenter, Richard W.; Lohman, Timothy G.; and Going, Scott B. "Relationship of Body Fat Percentage and Fat Distribution with Dehydroepiandrosterone Sulfate in Premenopausal Females." Journal of Clinical Endocrinology and Metabolism, 1993; 77(1):80-85.

19.   Wright, Jonathan V. "Physiological and Supraphysiological Suppression of Allergy by Dehydroepiandrosterone (DHEA): Effect and Possible Mechanism." International Clinical Nutrition Review, 1990; 10(3):392-395.

MAGNESIUM REFERENCE SOURCES

1. Altura, Bella T. and Altura, Burton M. "The Role of Magnesium in Etiology of Strokes and Cerebrovasospasm." Magnesium, 1982; 1:277-291.

2. Cox, I. M.; Campbell, M.J.; and Dowson, D. "Red Blood Cell Magnesium and Chronic Fatigue Syndrome." The Lancet, 1991; 337:757-760.

3. Editorial. "Is Magnesium the Miracle Weapon Against Cancer." Prevention, July 1968, pp. 16-17.

4. Gaby, Alan R. MAGNESIUM - HOW AN IMPORTANT MINERAL HELPS PREVENT HEART ATTACKS AND RELIEVE STRESS. Keats Publishing, New Canaan, Connecticut 1994.

5. Graham, L. A.; Caesar, J. J.; and Burgen, A.S.V. "Gastrointestinal Absorption and Excretion of Mg^{28} in Man." Metabolism, Clinical and Experimental, 1960; 9:646-659.

6. Gupta, J. Sen and Srivastavan, K.K. "Effect of Potassium-Magnesium Aspartate on Endurance Work in Man." Indian Journal of Experimental Biology, 1973; 11:392-394.

7. Henrotte, J.G. "Type A Behavior and Magnesium Metabolism." Magnesium, 1986; 5:201-210.

8. Higgins, George L. "Magnesium Medicine Comes of Age." Emergency Medicine, February 28, 1991, pp. 83-95.

9. Laban, E. and Charbon, G.A. "Magnesium and Cardiac Arrhythmias: Nutrient or Drug?" Journal of the American College of Nutrition, 1986; 5:521-532.

10. Levin, Barton S. and Coburn, Jack, W. (Editorial) "Magnesium, the Mimic/Antagonist of Calcium." The New England Journal of Medicine, 1984; 310(19):1253-1254.

11. Mauskop, A.; Altura, B.T.; Cracco, R. Q.; and Altura, B.M. "Deficiency in Serum Ionized Magnesium But Not Total Magnesium in Patients With Migraines. Possible Role of ICa^{2+}/IMg^{2+} Ratio." Headache, 1992; pp. 135-138.

12. Nielsen, Forrest H. "Studies on the Relationship Between Boron and Magnesium Which Possibly Affects the Formation and Maintenance of Bones." Magnesium Trace Elements, 1990; 9:61-69.

13. Reinhart, Richard A. "Magnesium Metabolism: A Review With Special Reference to the Relationship Between Intracellular Content and Serum Levels." Archives of Internal Medicine, 1988; 148:2415-2420

14. Romano, Thomas J. and Stiller, John W. "Magnesium Deficiency in Fibromyalgia Syndrome." Journal of Nutritional Medicine, 1994; 4:165-167.

15. Rude, Robert K. "Physiology of Magnesium
     Metabolism and the Important Role of Magnesium
     in Potassium Deficiency." The American Journal
     of Cardiology, 1989; 63:31G-34G.

16. Ryzen, Elisabeth; Elbaum, Nancy; Singer,
     Frederick R.; and Rude, Robert K. "Parenteral
     Magnesium Tolerance Testing in the Evaluation of
     Magnesium Deficiency[1]." Magnesium 1985;
     4:137-147.

17. Schendel, Diana E.; Berg, Cynthia J.; Yeargin-
     Allsopp, Marshalyn; Boyle, Coleen; and
     Decoufle, Pierre. "Prenatal Magnesium Sulfate
     Exposure and the Risk for Cerebral Palsy or
     Mental Retardation Among Very Low-Birth-
     Weight Children Aged 3 to 5 years." JAMA,
     1996; 276(22):1805-1810.

18. Seelig, Mildred. "Increased Need for Magnesium
     With the Use of Combined Oestrogen and
     Calcium for Osteoporosis Treatment."
     Magnesium Research, 1990; 3(3):197-215.

19. Seelig, Charles B. "Magnesium Deficiency in Two Hypertensive Patient Groups." Magnesium Deficiency 1990; 83(7):739-742.

20. Singh, R.B. and Cameron, E.A. (Letter to the Editor) "Relation of Myocardial Magnesium Deficiency to Sudden Death in Ischemic Heart Disease." American Heart Journal, 1982; 103(3):449-450.

21. Soriani, S.; Arnaldi, C.; De Carlo, L.; Acrudi, D.; Mazzotta, D.; Battistella, P.A.; Sartori, S.; and Abbasciano, V. "Serum and Red Blood Cell Magnesium Levels in Juvenile Migraine Patients." Headache, 1995; 35:14-16.

22. Turlapaty, Prasad D.M.V. and Altura, Burton M. "Magnesium Deficiency Produces Spasms of Coronary Arteries: Relationship to Etiology of Sudden Death Ischemic Heart Disease." Science, 1980; 208:198-200.

23. Welch, K.M. "Low Brain Magnesium in Migraine." Headache, 1989; 29(7):416-419.

24. Zonszein, Joel. "Magnesium and Diabetes." Practical Diabetology, 1991; 10(2):1-5.

PHOTOS

1. THE STONE lying on laminar crystals - the YINERGY™ source.

2. Three minute time exposure, in the dark, of the laminar crystal.

3. Jim Carter - Discoverer of the YINERGY™ concept.

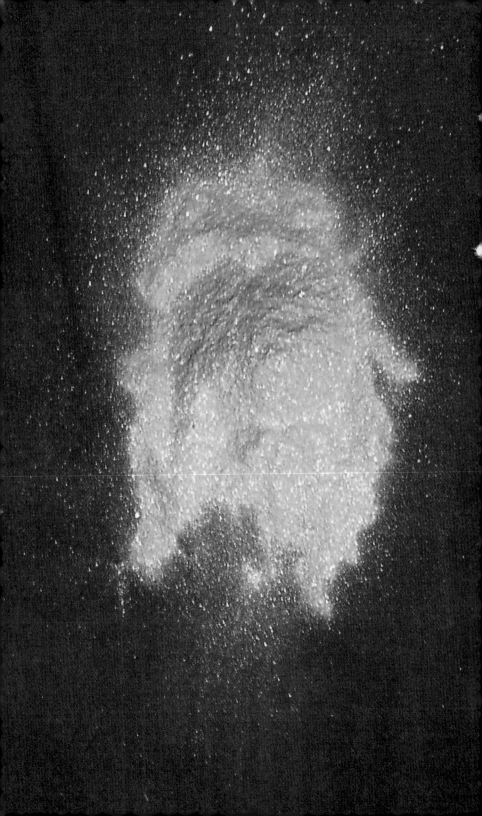